The Complete Guide to
Religious Education Volunteers

THE COMPLETE GUIDE TO RELIGIOUS EDUCATION VOLUNTEERS

DONALD RATCLIFF AND BLAKE J. NEFF

with chapters by Harold William Burgess
and James Michael Lee

Religious Education Press
Birmingham, Alabama

Library of Congress Cataloging-in-Publication Data

Ratcliff, Donald.
    The complete guide to religious education volunteers / Donald
Ratcliff and Blake J. Neff, with chapters by Harold William Burgess and
James Michael Lee.
    Includes bibliographical references and indexes.
    ISBN 0-89135-089-6
    1. Christian education.   2. Voluntarism—Religious aspects-
-Christianity.   I. Neff, Blake J.
BV1471.2.R37   1993
268'.3—dc20   92-38908
                                                                    CIP

Religious Education Press
5316 Meadow Brook Road
Birmingham, Alabama 35242
10 9 8 7 6 5 4 3 2

Religious Education Press publishes books exclusively in religious education and in areas closely related to religious education. It is committed
to enhancing and professionalizing religious education through the publication of serious, significant, and scholarly works.

PUBLISHER TO THE PROFESSION

Contents

Part I

Introducing Religious Education Volunteerism

Chapter One

What Is a Volunteer?

HAROLD WILLIAM BURGESS

One of the most urgent needs today in the church is volunteers. Recently *Christianity Today* emphasized that the decline in the number of Sunday schools is largely due to the lack of volunteers. As will be detailed later in this book, church researcher George Barna notes that the use of volunteers in the future will be quite different because of changes in the population. Churches that fail to note and adapt to these changes may find themselves without volunteers in the future. Yet volunteers have provided the basis for many church ministries since the beginning of the church. We are indeed in a crisis situation. We need to know more about volunteers.

Defining Volunteerism

It may be helpful to consider the concept of "volunteer" in relation to the idea of "professional." But, as is quickly evident, these concepts are not easy to relate because both suffer from a number of connotations that have grown out of our culturally conditioned use of these words. For example, it is easy to think of a volunteer as one who does menial work cheaply whereas it is costly to employ a professional. It should not be surprising that such cultural connotations muddy our understanding of the conditions under which volunteers can contribute most fruitfully to religious enterprises.

What Is a Professional? A professional is an individual who: (1) has mastered a theory (or set of interrelated theories) and (2) employs this theory in practice (3) for meaningful compensation (i.e., a living wage).

Accordingly, professional training commonly begins with a theory that informs one's activity. Training also involves the development of appropriate skills that enable one to practice the designated theory. Finally, this training typically culminates in a certificate granting professional status. Such a certificate implies that the person will be paid for what they do.

It is worth remembering that professionals are valued more for their competence and leadership than for their labor alone. This point is illustrated by a story about a mechanic who was called to fix a machine that would not run. The mechanic looked carefully over the machine, thought for a while, then tapped on a bearing three times with a small hammer. Immediately the machine began to run perfectly. However, the owner objected to the repair bill, claiming that $500.00 was far too much to pay anyone for tapping three times with a hammer. A second bill arrived in a few days. This one was itemized: (1) for tapping with hammer, $10.00; (2) for knowing where to tap, $490.00.

Then too, professionals must continue their training to upgrade their theoretical knowledge and skills. In such continued training, it is expected that professionals will learn in two ways. Some new learning is related to existing perspectives (assimilation), whereas other learning requires new paradigms (accommodation) and occasionally the discarding of old ideas. Assimilative learning generally is not painful. It often gives one the feeling of having learned much as one's cup, so to speak, is filled. Accommodative learning, on the other hand, often brings the kind of learning pain that some developmental psychologists have labeled "disequilibration." In this case one's cup is not being filled so much as being replaced. I well remember going to a plastic surgeon's office and being upset that he was out of town. I had an ugly, and potentially lethal, lesion on my nose. Noting my distress, the nurse said, "I hope you realize that it is in your best interests for the doctor to learn the best new ways of thinking and continually to upgrade his skills." Now, every time I look in a mirror, I am thankful for the up-to-date theoretical knowledge and finely honed skills of that very competent surgeon.

We live in a world that is characterized by change. Most people would be quite happy if they could be absolutely assured that their way of looking at things would never have to be altered in any way. Unfortunately, such assurances do not seem to exist. Professionals in the religious education arena must learn to learn in all necessary ways, including accommodative learning. With confidence one can predict a smaller and more bounded ministry for any who will not grow. Attempting to minister in the environment of a changing world without growth will not yield professionalism; in fact such an attitude leads to loneliness and, possibly, anger.

Volunteers: A Need to Bless and Be Blessed

Why do individuals volunteer for tasks that bring no financial reward and sometimes even bring criticism? The research on volunteers suggests clearly that the twin answers are that volunteers possess a deep desire to bless others and, second, a desire to be blessed. In other words volunteers normally need to be of benefit to others and, though few would put it in so bald a fashion, they need to feel they have benefited.

A number of related questions are addressed by others throughout this book. How do we encourage the right kind of volunteering? What task dimensions work best for the volunteer community? Reflecting upon these matters creates a growing conviction that *it is unconscionable for us to seek volunteers until religious education professionals are committed to grow as professionals.* In this case, a professional might best be thought of as "one who possesses a theory that can be practiced—and shared."

Most professionals are very willing to accept paychecks. No one argues that it is not professional to receive a paycheck. But also the professional community has a responsibility to create a meaningful theoretical structure within which the volunteer community can bless and be blessed. The commander of a U.S. Navy base made this point succinctly: "When I was a volunteer lay reader aboard ship, my service could have been a greater blessing to the ship's crew, and it could have been more rewarding to me, had I been privileged to have been given the professional training that such an important task seems to require."

Six Benefits of Using Volunteers

Volunteers are blessed through the service of giving, which in turn blesses others. In addition, however, the religious community itself is blessed by volunteers in at least six important ways.

1. Employing volunteers combats the dreaded "spectator syndrome" that curses so many religious communities. Many individuals have not been genuinely employed in their respective religious communities but faithfully attend all kinds of meetings. Such individuals can often be identified by their body language. As they slump in their seats, they seem to say, "Well here I am, preacher (or teacher), thrill me with your sermon, your liturgy, your lecture — make me feel religious."

Such persons are reminiscent of the television "short" developed by the

Brethren and Mennonite churches, wherein a first century Christian is shoved into the Roman arena. A lion comes bounding across the turf and leaps, knocking the silent Christian back into the camera. The picture breaks up into "snow," as the audience hears the lion breaking the Christian's bones. At this point a voice says: "Christianity didn't used to be a spectator sport—it still isn't."

2. Religious institutions need volunteers to thrive, if not to survive. Religious communities simply do not operate effectively lacking volunteers. One night of my life was spent on a Texas ranch in an immense house that seemed to stretch in each direction for several blocks. The host was my stereotype of a Texan. He told the following Texas story. "There is an interesting church on the other side of that hill." He pointed out of the picture window and across a rolling field. "Oil was struck on the property. They closed the membership and now pay dividends. The church doesn't need any volunteers. They hire outsiders to do everything that needs to be done. Something's wrong, though, it isn't what you'd think a church ought to be." I've told this story a few times, once where someone knew the rest of the story. He told me that the story was true. "The church," he said, "never got any better. It is as dead today as when they closed the membership."

3. Volunteers bring wholeness to the religious education professional. As James Dittes reminds us, religious professionals are often psychologically crippled persons. He may be right. Henri Nouwen agrees with him, as does David Moberg. Volunteers can be a genuine blessing to professionals who have much to gain from working with "real people." Involvement with volunteers promotes growth and wholeness. Volunteers have done much to sharpen the skills and bring beauty into an otherwise misshapen professional community.

4. Using volunteers brings wholeness to the church community. Roy Zuck is just one of many writers who have demonstrated that a key reason for dropping out of church, or any other religious community, is the "feeling of not being used. Hence, the feeling of being useless." James Michael Lee helps make the same point in his writings on faith. "To keep faith hot," he suggests, "it has to be lived out." When it comes to volunteers, the slogan, "use 'em or lose 'em," tells it all.

5. Volunteerism provides meaningful self investment. Investment of one's self is an underemployed concept in a culture that sets the priority on cash value. We give our money but keep our selves in reserve. Constructive use of volunteers is an effective means of providing them a way to give something of what they are. This is a concept that may have

far-reaching implications in light of a recent research project in Jacksonville, Florida. The Jacksonville study tentatively found that persons who volunteer to give time have significantly less heart trouble than those who give only money. While this finding did not claim to have established a cause-effect relationship, nor has it as yet been substantiated through replication, this finding is certainly worth thinking about.

6. Deployment of volunteers is perhaps the most effective means of addressing the varied kinds of religious needs represented in any community. One Detroit minister found that volunteers seemed to give more effective help to individuals struggling to overcome alcohol addiction than did professional counselors. Isaiah (58) seems to have envisioned volunteers as a major resource in the rebuilding of shattered cities.

Volunteers can be a great asset to any Christian organization. Specifically, they are usually an important aspect of religious education in church and parachurch organizations. Throughout biblical and church history volunteers have contributed regularly to the effective ministry of the church, as will be seen in the next chapter.

For Further Reading

Dittes, James. *Minister on the Spot*. Philadelphia: Pilgrim, 1970, pp. 23-38.

Lee, James Michael, ed. *Handbook of Faith*. Birmingham, Ala: Religious Education Press, 1990, see especially pp. 264-302.

Moberg, David O. *The Church as a Social Institution*, revised edition. Grand Rapids, Mich.: Baker, 1984, see especially pp. 481-511.

Nouwen, Henri J. M. *The Wounded Healer: Ministry in Contemporary Society*. Garden City, N.J.: Image, 1979, see especially pp. 81-98.

Stafford, Tim. "This Little Light of Mine." *Christianity Today* (8 October 1990), pp. 29-32.

Zuck, Roy B., and Gene Getz. *Christian Youth, An In-depth Study*. Chicago: Moody, 1968, see especially pp. 156-163.

Chapter Two

Biblical Roots of Volunteerism

Both the Old and New Testaments emphasize volunteerism. Volunteerism is also to be found throughout church history. Clearly this is an often overlooked aspect of the Christian faith.

The Old Testament

The long tradition of volunteerism first appears in the Old Testament when Noah received the call from God and built the boat. The message, repeated many times and in many ways in the Bible, is that those who follow God must volunteer to help meet needs. Noah only helped his family, but he attempted to reach out to everyone in his community. Volunteers may not be able to help everyone they would like, but their talents need to be focused on those who can be helped. The boat, a picture of the church meeting together, is not a place to reside permanently. It may not be a place in which we are altogether content (surely Noah must have complained about the smell!). Rather our boat, the church, prepares us for life in a world we are to help change. Modern day Noahs, motivated by Christian compassion, also need to focus their efforts on reaching and teaching about the kingdom of God. And, like Noah, we must help meet the religious and social needs of those around us.

The "Lone Ranger" mentality has too often invaded God's people; the belief that one can do it all alone without help from others. In the eighteenth chapter of Exodus we see Moses attempting to resolve the many disputes among the Israelites. Jethro, his wife's father, advised him to get some help by calling on volunteers. Yet today, many attempt to follow the example of Moses by trying to do everything themselves. They, too, need a Jethro that will encourage them to recruit and train volunteers for doing the work, rather than trying to do it all alone. Even the Lone Ranger had Tonto to help!

The value of volunteerism is seen throughout the Old Testament. In Deuteronomy 14 we see the Hebrews commanded to save the tithe for three years. This percentage of income was to be given to the Levite, the religious leader who did not have personal land or inheritance. But the tithe was also used for the sojourner (the wanderer or homeless), the fatherless (the orphan which today might include children of the divorced), and the widow (perhaps including women that are estranged from their husbands through divorce, abandonment, abuse, alcoholism, and so on). These people, says Deuteronomy, are to "eat and be filled; that the Lord your God may bless you in all the work of your hands that you do" (14:29). Our efforts and funds must provide nourishment (physical, emotional, spiritual) for the needy. The idea is service without thought of payment, except for God's blessing.

The remainder of the Old Testament has numerous examples of volunteers who served without thought of return. Sometimes the Old Testament volunteers had to be "drafted." Certainly the volunteer prophets encouraged others also to volunteer by their messages of concern for the needy. We can read countless commands by these spiritual giants to help the exploited and the poor. A strong foundation for volunteerism is laid in the Old Testament.

The New Testament

Jesus volunteered. He voluntarily became a servant to provide us with an example of what God expects. Philippians 2:7-8 describes the Son of God lowering, or emptying himself, so that he could become the servant of humankind. He had compassion on others (Mt 9:36), which moved him to teach, to heal, and to deliver others from their problems. He took the time to show personal concern for the person who was ignored by others, such as the woman at the well and the Gadarian demoniac.

Christ quoted the prophet Isaiah in describing his ministry: "The Spirit of the Lord is upon me, because he has anointed me to preach good news to the poor. He has sent me to proclaim release to the captives and recovering of sight to the blind, to set at liberty those who are oppressed, to proclaim the acceptable year of the Lord" (Lk 4:18-19). This details many of the activities of modern volunteers.

Volunteers show concern for the poor, reaching out to those in need. But the poor also need social nurturing so they can escape poverty. They usually need education, including religious education, so that new values can be instilled. One of the reasons the English revival under John Wesley succeeded was that he emphasized the spiritual, educational, social, and physical needs of the poor.

"Release to the captives" is both spiritual and literal. Emotional release comes to those in prison by volunteers showing their concern through visitation and advocacy. But those imprisoned by adverse situations also need to be set free. Religious education releases people from the captivity of ignorance about matters of faith.

Recovery of sight to the blind again can be both literal and symbolic. Volunteers may help those without sight gain skills, such as the use of braille. Volunteers may record books on cassette tape for the blind. Because of a dearth of religious material for the blind, providing tapes and training may, in a sense, help the blind to see again. But many who read this passage also see the social and religious blindness of people. Many throughout the world have eyes that function perfectly, yet fail to comprehend religious truths and biblical content. Blindness to faith occurs because they have never been exposed to that faith, because they lack interest, or because of misconceptions about religious faith. Volunteers in the church can help those without sight begin to see the truth.

Liberty for the oppressed is a key concern for many theologians today. Oppression reigns in many areas of the world, regardless of the political orientation of those in control. Christians should bring about liberty for the politically oppressed, the emotionally oppressed, and the financially oppressed.

The final phrase Jesus used to describe his ministry (and thus our ministry as his followers) is "proclaiming the acceptable year of the Lord." This refers to the year of Jubilee, a once in every fifty years celebration when all debts are canceled, a time of great rejoicing. Volunteerism may help people cancel their spiritual debts, their physical debts, and their emotional debts to others. Volunteers share in the jubilee by paying some of their indebtedness to society and perhaps even help compensate for wrongs they have committed by making restitution through their service. Those who give of their time often receive great joy from their efforts, constituting a celebration of jubilee among volunteers.

Not only was Jesus a volunteer, he also called volunteers. We must never forget that the disciples were volunteers, who responded without compulsion or payment, who were trained, then imitated their master, and later volunteered to take on the task of leading the church. The disciples served others, at the Lord's command, when they passed out food to the hungry and healed the sick.

We also see the disciples, and later the seventy, being volunteers when they were sent out for "practice ministry" (Lk 9 & 10). Their two tasks (9:2, 10:9) were to preach the kingdom and heal the sick. These tasks constitute the basic thrust of religious education — telling others and helping others. The disciples functioned as volunteers, both talking and doing. They traveled light, without staff, bag, bread, or money. We too must be disciple volunteers who travel light but who focus on teaching and healing those who need instruction or who suffer.

The parable of the Good Samaritan shows volunteerism in its ideal form. It also indicates that good, well-meaning religious people can, like the Levite and priest, ignore the genuine needs of those around them while concentrating on the prescribed tasks on their agendas. The Samaritan, in contrast, took the time to evaluate the actual need, brought his resources to bear on that need, and then recruited outside assistance as it was needed. The parables of the Good Samaritan provides a captivating picture of volunteerism and volunteer leadership.

Paul, in several New Testament passages (Eph 4, 1 Cor 12, Rom 12), describes an analogy for the church. The human body, with all of its various parts, is like the church in that each person has a distinctive function. Unlike the human body, God's people are not automatically tied together and unified, but the analogy reminds us that we *should* be united. For the body to be effective, each part must do its job, its respective function. Without volunteers, working cooperatively and harmoniously, the body (the church) cannot be body-like. The body serves the head's commands, and our head (Christ) has commanded that we be concerned with others.

1 Peter 2:9 describes all Christians as ministers, or priests. Everyone that is a member of the church does the work of the ministry, not just a few paid clergy. This idea, often affirmed by Protestants, was also underscored by the Vatican II document on the laity and reaffirmed in detail by the Bishops Committee at their 1980 annual meeting in Washington. The Vatican II document stated, "The laity derive the right and obligation to the apostolate from their very union with Christ . . . They are consecrated for the royal priesthood." Church leaders are to prepare others to do the ministry; they should find, train, encourage, and otherwise guide the laity in volunteer ministry. Laity must renounce a purely spectator role and take on a volunteerism role. We must minister through service, the central thrust of volunteerism in a Christian context.

Ephesians 4:12 states that gifts are given to each person in the church "for the equipping of the saints for the work of service, to the building up of the body of Christ." Serving is central to the task of the Christian, and central to spiritual growth. Like everyone else, Christians learn best by doing not just hearing (Jas 1:22).

Spiritual gifts exist within the context of service to others, never just for self-centered preoccupation (1 Pt 4:10). Spiritual gifts are to be used voluntarily in Christian service, indeed service is the reason for having gifts. Mary Schramm states: "Many people find the best use of their gifts does not coincide with how they earn their paycheck. The sense of unfulfillment, caused by that creative being inside us, needs attention . . . It may be in our leisure hours that we engage in the kind of ministry where we feel free to express our gifts."

Dozens of times throughout the New Testament the early Christians described themselves as "servants," those who serve God and others. Voluntarily serving is the result of Christian love (Gal 5:13), a key indication that one has become a Christian (Jn 15:12, 1 Jn 4). Indeed Christ noted that caring for the needs of others was involved in eternal destiny (Mt 16:17, 25:31-46). Jesus stated that volunteer ministry, even to the least important person, was credited as service for God and would receive glory as a result. We must begin to see Christ in those we serve through volunteerism, because in some mystical way by serving the neighbor we also serve Christ.

Volunteerism Throughout Church History

Following the New Testament era, the practice of volunteer social and teaching ministry continued. The local church, which met in homes until about A.D. 200, continued as the locus of religious learning and charitable outreach for Christians. Those involved in these efforts were primarily volunteers, people who served without payment.

This tradition continued, within the context of a more organized church, during the Middle Ages. Hospitals and foundling homes developed as a result of Christian concern for the unfortunate, often staffed by workers who received little or nothing for their efforts. Monasteries became centers for healing, instruction, care for the mentally ill, and provision for the poor. Those who followed St. Francis of Assissi did more than volunteer their time; they also volunteered all of their possessions for the sake of others.

The Pietistic movement in the 1700s also produced concern for the needy. Schools, clinics, and orphanages were established, and deplorable prison and asylum conditions were changed for the better. Beneficial child labor laws and the end of slavery can be directly traced to the efforts of volunteers. The Sunday school movement developed in which Christian volunteers taught children to read on Sunday, using the Bible and religious books as curriculum. The first Sunday schools were all-day efforts, not just an hour on Sunday morning. Today, in response to widespread reading deficiencies a rebirth of the original concept of Sunday school is developing outside the church in adult volunteer staff literacy centers. We also see volunteerism countless times as an outgrowth of the Social Gospel movement of the early 1900s, as well as in rescue missions and many church and parachurch agencies that developed.

Volunteerism has both a strong biblical and historical basis in the church. Perhaps it can be said that the church is at its best when there is a strong volunteerism spirit, where people serve without thought of personal reward. A wide variety of church and parachurch related ministries need volunteers today. In the next chapter we will survey the broad spectrum of those ministries before turning to the main thrust of this book, volunteers in religious education ministry.

For Further Reading

Bannon, William, and Suzanne Donovan. *Volunteers and Ministry*. Ramsey, N.J.: Paulist, 1983.

Christie, Les. *How to Recruit and Train Volunteer Youth Workers*. Grand Rapids, Mich: Zondervan, 1992. [Previously released under the title *Unsung Heroes*.]

Foster, Charles. *The Ministry of the Volunteer Teacher*. Nashville: Abingdon, 1986.

Roadcup, David. *Recruiting, Training, and Developing Volunteer Youth Workers*. Cincinnati: Standard, 1987.

Schram, Mary. *Gifts of Grace*. Minneapolis: Augsburg, 1982.

Chapter Three

The Broad Spectrum
of Church Volunteerism

Volunteerism in the church is a broad, multifaceted area at the present time. Indeed the majority of tasks in many churches are accomplished through the use of volunteers. Before we concentrate upon volunteerism in religious education, an examination of the broad variety of volunteers in the church will give us an appreciation for the essential nature of volunteers. We also will examine some of the difficulties often encountered in volunteer efforts.

A Survey of Volunteers in the Church

What do volunteers do in the church? Perhaps the most public jobs stand out. The elders (or an equivalent position) in most churches usually volunteer for their positions. While they may be elected or appointed, there must be a willingness to give freely of their time to take that elected or appointed position. Sometimes these leaders will serve as guest speakers, delivering a message to the congregation when the pastor is absent or ill. Recently the Roman Catholic church has increasingly relied upon similar lay individuals to lead the church when no priest is available.

Speaking engagements outside the local church by laity also bear mentioning. The church or some ministry of the church may be presented by interested members on a volunteer basis. One church invited a team of volunteers from another local church in the area to describe their experiences on a two-week overseas mission. The resultant igniting of interest produced a new team of overseas volunteers.

The choir members in many churches volunteer. The music director in smaller churches is often an unpaid volunteer position. Members of the church may volunteer their musical talents for a special musical performance.

Less obvious is the work of volunteer church administrators who oversee, and often do, many of the necessary tasks of keeping the program going. Decisions must be made, discussions held, and appointments to positions made by such volunteers.

The church secretary is increasingly a paid position. But in many smaller churches, no official secretary exists other than someone who gives a few hours a week to typing, copying, and other essential secretarial tasks. Several supportive volunteers may take on the tasks of a secretary, each giving one or more hours a week to this job.

Visitation is an important aspect of church work. Visitors and new members often need the personal touch of a home visit. A personal call may mean the difference between being a once-in-a-lifetime visit or repeated attendance at a church. It also may help the occasional visitor become a regular participant in the church. While the pastor/s may take on the bulk of the visitation task in small churches, involving volunteers in visitation can be a part of an active lay ministry.

Churches often use volunteers in work camps and youth camps, as counselors and other workers. Volunteers often build churches and other needed buildings in poor communities in the United States and overseas. First-hand involvement in these activities can be an enriching experience for volunteers.

Parachurch groups also make extensive use of volunteers. Child Evangelism Fellowship is a broad network of individuals who take time each week to talk to children about religious matters. Sometimes released time programs, where children are taken out of school for part of the school day for religious activities, are staffed by one or more volunteers.

These, and many other religious activities, rely heavily upon volunteers. While religious education can take place in several of the above situations, most people tend to consider the focus of religious education as being in one of two contexts: church teaching and small groups in homes. In most cases, volunteers are used a great deal in these contexts as well.

In the church, Sunday school and CCD teachers usually volunteer. Bible clubs, sometimes divided by gender, are commonly held on Sunday evenings or another evening of the week. The spectrum of such ministry is diverse, from the youngest to oldest attenders, and sometimes divided according to personal interests. During the regular church service volunteers may lead a junior church program for children. Nursery workers, while not usually considered teachers, are indeed helping infants and toddlers learn that the church is a happy, pleasant place to stay on Sundays (or conversely that the church is less than a happy place). Education is not just mental learning but also emotional and affective learning (and this is true for older children, teens, and adults just as much as the toddlers and infants).

Small groups in the church have become increasingly popular over the last ten to twenty years. Many church leaders consider this area crucial to the church. The most successful megachurches generally have a small group ministry as the backbone of the church, even though the casual attender may not recognize that fact. These small groups may be primarily for cognitive learning (such as Bible study groups or catechal groups), fellowship oriented, or centered upon worship. Each of these can be educational in some sense and thus be a volunteer ministry in religious education. One must not overlook the ministry of family members to one another as well, another "small group" in the home!

The scope of volunteerism can be summarized in the diagram on the next page. The categories and diagram were inspired by the work of James Anderson, Ezra Jones, William Bannon, and Suzanne Donovan, although nearly all of the listed functions and categories are unique to the book you are reading.

Obstacles to Volunteer Ministry

Such a broad range of volunteer ministry often meets with difficulties. Marlene Wilson has noted several problems in volunteer ministries in the church. First she notes that there is a lack of clear definition of most volunteer ministries. Rarely do you find job descriptions for such positions, producing confusion about expectations for both volunteers and others in the church.

Second, tradition often interferes with new ideas and perspectives. "We've always done it this way" limits creativity and often transforms new converts into pew-sitters or drives them away.

Sometimes churches survey their congregations for interests and talents but then do not use those talents and interests. The message is conveyed to potential volunteers that they are not needed. Perhaps it would be better if surveys were not used at all, if no action results.

Delegation is sometimes difficult for church leaders. The purpose of volunteer ministry is to share the work in the church, but if leaders cannot delegate, volunteers may have little or nothing to do. Perhaps just as often, what is delegated to volunteers is considered insignificant and peripheral to the church, providing little motivation for volunteers to participate.

TRIANGLE OF VOLUNTEER FUNCTIONS

INTERPERSONAL

1. Home & hospital visitation
2. Evangelism
3. Fellowship planning
4. Soup kitchen/shut-in meals
5. Recreational ministry
6. Other community outreach & witness
7. Other social ministry

ORGANIZATIONAL

1. Planning/organization
2. Budgeting
3. Record keeping/clerical work
4. Fund drives
5. Newsletter writing/editing
6. Building maintenance
7. Other committees/activities

Volunteer
Tasks

Spiritual

SPIRITUAL

1. Children's, youth & adult leadership
2. Pulpit supply
3. Liturgical ministry
4. Prayer & music
5. Peer counseling
6. Discipleship/spiritual development program
7. Other religious ministry

Very often churches give more attention to the jobs available than to the people who volunteer. Though the open positions are often the most salient aspect of the church for leaders, a better approach is to consider the talents and gifts of the volunteer first. What is the best ministry for the volunteer? Does your church have such a ministry? For too long churches have tried to put square pegs in round holes and then are amazed when things do not work out. This problem is compounded by how difficult it is for some volunteers to describe their abilities, their interest (and lack of interest) in some jobs, areas where they want to learn and grow, the timing of breaks from the job, and so on. The problems, though sometimes difficult, are not insurmountable. Many of these difficulties will be considered later in this book.

Case Studies of Religious Volunteerism

To illustrate volunteerism within religious contexts, five specific case studies will be cited. These are chosen to indicate how wide the spectrum is in volunteer ministry. One can make a case for each of these being related to religious education.

Case 1 — Roving Volunteers. RVICS stands for Roving Volunteers in Christ's Service, an organization with headquarters in Orlando, Florida. These volunteers are retired individuals who live most of the year in recreational vehicles (thus the double meaning of the "RV" in RVICS) and travel throughout the United States and sometimes overseas providing physical labor for religious colleges, camps, childrens homes, and other Christian organizations.

Generally a group of several families, each with a recreational vehicle, will stay at a location for three to four weeks. Each family is financially self-sufficient, living on retirement income, and thus the only expense to the religious organization is the materials needed to accomplish tasks and provision of a lot with hookups for the recreational vehicles.

The day begins with a devotional time among the RVICS members (a Bible study also is held each week). The men in the group work three and one-half days each week on manual tasks provided by the host organization. This may involve pouring cement for sidewalks, repairing buildings, and other tasks for which the men are skilled. Wives generally work half of the day on secretarial tasks, sewing, mailings, and in general assisting in areas where they are needed. The other half day involves personal housekeeping and visiting among the RVICS group.

Participation involves a three-month commitment at a time, although that three months can be spaced throughout a year if desired. Individuals must apply prior to age seventy. There is little publicity about RVICS; participants generally learn about the program through word of mouth.

In speaking to several of the RVICS participants, they emphasized the enjoyment of traveling but also the desire to be of service to others. They especially appreciated the combining of ministry with close fellowship in the small group and traveling. Since members of each group motivate one another, discouragement is reportedly uncommon. All those interviewed described the unpleasant prospect of nothing to do during retirement and that RVICS provided real meaning and purpose. They also described the incentive of seeing genuine results from their activities, as well as opportunities to speak to people about their faith.

The RVICS headquarters keeps track of details for tax purposes. There is a lengthy application process and sometimes interviews are required for participation. A newsletter is produced by the headquarters as well as each group. At the time of the interview there were 450 projects and 230 RVICS participants in the fourteen-year-old program.

Case 2 — A Church Program. This case study was reported by a participant in a small church of eighty members. A central feature of the religious education program was a master teacher always available to those involved in the religious education program. Volunteers were trained in an extensive preservice program, regular inservice training sessions, and weekly fifteen minute follow-up discussions with the master teacher every Sunday afternoon.

Preservice training involved eight to ten classes, two hours each, leading to certification for teaching. These classes concentrated upon the particular age range in which the volunteer teacher specialized. Details of making a lesson plan were taught systematically, and a month of lesson plans were required before the first teaching assignment. Participants were pretested prior to preservice training. Instruction included modeling of a lesson taught at the specific age level. They were then required to develop part of a lesson and eventually wrote an entire lesson. These training classes were highly desired by many in the church, and a number of individuals took several series of lessons so they could teach at multiple age levels. Prospective teachers were evaluated subsequent to the training and were required to reach minimal levels of competence before assignment to a class.

Religious educators were not allowed to keep a Sunday school booklet in their classes, because this was thought to delimit spontaneity and perhaps foster lack of preparation. Teachers were also encouraged to have many outside contacts with those they taught. Children were evaluated in the content learned through the use of games.

Workers involved in the program signed a "worker's covenant" for one year. Those who volunteered had to be screened and approved by the religious education committee of the church.

The program was very popular, even though public presentations of the process emphasized the requirement of extensive training and monitoring. Participants stated that while the program was appealing, the personality of the coordinator also was a vital part of the program's popularity.

While this case study departs from the ideal of professionals doing most of the teaching, as described in chapter four and elsewhere in this book, it is suggestive of an acceptable volunteer program for small churches that cannot afford paid professionals but still want quality religious education.

Case 3 — Laity Care. In his doctoral dissertation James Davies examined three long-term care ministries led by volunteer laity. All had been deemed successful ministries by seminary professors and by general reputation in other churches. Each had operated continuously for at least six years.

One of the programs involved intimate sharing to meet emotional, physical, and spiritual needs of members. Activities included socials, Bible study, outreach activities, and prayer services. The groups varied in size from five to sixteen. They met weekly in homes, with attendance based upon geographic location. Training to lead a group included nine video cassettes, eleven hours of audio cassettes, and reading a 133 page notebook.

A second church involved volunteer laity in small groups to provide one-to-one ministry for those in crisis situations or needing general support. Twenty-six sessions, once a week, covering 1200 pages of information, comprised the training. These volunteer caregivers received the names of people needing help from the church. The program was coordinated by two part-time staff members, each giving ten hours of supervision.

The third program described by Davies involved age-graded clusters, not geographic clusters, as the basis for involvement. The purpose was meeting for discipleship, care, worship, and evangelism. Instead of a small group context, lay care took place in adult Sunday school classes of seventy-five to a hundred individuals. A twenty-five page manual was used for training, which occurred in classes led by members of the church steering committee.

From these three different approaches for lay care, Davies found five key factors common to each, thought to contribute to success:

1. Strong commitment marked the participants and the sponsoring churches.

2. Training involved "personal enrichment" and enhancement of performance skills.

3. Flexibility existed so that adjustments could be made as the programs progressed; they were modified with a priority placed on meeting participants' needs.

4. Leaders showed respect and care for volunteers and participants, producing a genuine team approach.

5. Support was provided through encouragement and monitoring of volunteers' activities.

Case 4 — Released Time. Released time instruction is the practice of releasing children or teenagers from public school for one or more hours a week, to receive religious education during regular school hours. By law they must receive religious instruction at a church or other location off school grounds. This form of religious education has been supported by Supreme Court decisions since the 1950s. The religious education provided varies from catechism classes for Roman Catholics, to Bible verse memorization led by fundamentalists, to doctrinal courses for Jews, to counseling or studying popular topics (e.g., values in dating) led by moderate Baptists.

Ken Wright, a prominent leader in released time, when interviewed noted that the majority of released time instructors are volunteers, primarily retired teachers and housewives. Administrators, fund raisers, and those who coordinate the programs with schools are usually volunteers as well. One man took early retirement from the Army to direct a released time program rather than take up a new career.

Many of the volunteers are involved year after year, particularly those who work with elementary aged children. What keeps them involved? Wright emphasizes their strong sense of ownership, feeling the program is theirs, an attitude accentuated by the need for personal creativity (most programs avoid a standardized curriculum). Volunteers do not see themselves as "dishing out predigested material," but rather as innovators who are reaching youngsters that might otherwise never hear about religious faith. Wright notes that programs offered by Christians tend to work best if they are ecumenical and if they are supported by ministers and key community civic groups.

Case 5 — Transforming a Life. Volunteers involved in religious ministry do not always work within an extensive program; even one-to-one ministry can be very effective. For example, a businesswoman discovered that a man in his mid-twenties had been convicted of multiple DUI incidents (driving while under the influence of alcohol) and as a result was sentenced to several months in jail. He also had a long record of troublesome behavior. Since she had known him as a boy, she asked the local judge if she could have custody of the man during the day so he could work with her husband doing manual labor. The judge agreed to the experiment, noting it was highly irregular. The judge had so much confidence in the businesswoman he gave no rules for the arrangement except that the man was required to follow the businesswoman's instructions.

Each day the man was picked up at the jail, taken to work, and then returned each evening. He also attended church with the businesswoman and her husband three times a week. They helped him become involved in the church basketball team. The couple brought the man into their home many evenings to share meals, watch television, and discuss matters of faith. They remarked that he had become "like one of the family." They stood by him when he had conflicts with others but were also firm in establishing guidelines.

Four weeks later he appeared before the judge. There were many indications he had changed a great deal: He had a more controlled temper, he no longer complained as much, he talked a great deal more, and he no longer used alcohol. The judge released him to live with his parents, but he continued to work for the businesswoman and attend church. Over the following weeks his family continually remarked to the woman and her husband about how much the man had changed and that he was avoiding old friends who sometimes got him into trouble. At last report he had made an affirmation of faith and his family had begun attending church with him. The businesswoman and her husband indicated that they would like to repeat the experiment with another individual because of the great satisfaction they feel from the results.

Overt Religious Education

Most of this book will concentrate upon religious education volunteerism in a focused, rather than broader sense. In other words, we will generally emphasize the overt teaching of religion in a variety of contexts. While the indirect learning that takes place in situations such as social action projects is clearly an important aspect of religious education, and many comments in this book may apply to that situation as well, the focus will be teaching religion more directly.

To a great extent, religious education with volunteers is like any good religious education. A number of the chapters of this book will parallel the general topics of religious education. However, we will focus repeatedly on the distinctives of using *volunteers* in religious education ministry.

It might be noted that teaching is often considered a gift. Some people seem to be born teachers. At the very least, some have more potential than others. By this assumption, we also must admit that some simply cannot teach. They are probably gifted in another way. Between those who are gifted in teaching, and those who have no potential for teaching, are the vast majority who have potential that must be carefully nurtured. These people may have to work hard to learn the skills of good teaching, yet can become effective volunteers with the right training.

For Further Reading

Anderson, James, and Ezra Jones. *The Management of Ministry.* New York: Harper & Row, 1978.

Bannon, William, and Suzanne Donovan. *Volunteers and Ministry.* New York: Paulist, 1983.

Davies, James. *Factors Contributing to Successful, Long-Term Laity Care Ministries.* Doctor of Education Dissertation, University of Georgia, Athens, Ga., 1989. Also see his article by the same title, *Christian Education Journal* 12 (1992), pp. 119-130.

Wilson, Marlene. *How to Mobilize Church Volunteers.* Minneapolis: Augsburg, 1983.

Wright, Ken. Personal interview. Toccoa, Ga., 27 November 1991. [Ken is the editor of the only known journal on released time religious education and is an active leader in the national association.]

Chapter Four

Religious Education Volunteers Are Very Special

JAMES MICHAEL LEE

Introduction

There are many kinds of church work open to laypersons today. Of all these forms of church work, religious education stands above the rest because of its uniqueness.

The basic reasons for the inherent superiority of religious education as compared to other church activities are threefold. First, Jesus expressly and unequivocally designated religious education activity as absolutely essential for the fulfillment of the church's mission. Second, Jesus was primarily a religious educator, and therefore laypersons who take on the religious education role walk more closely in the footsteps of the master than is possible in any other ministry fully open to laypersons. Third, religious education work requires a greater degree of competency from its facilitators than does the enactment of other ministries in the church. It is the combination of these three factors which makes religious education work preeminent among all other church activities and ministries available to laypersons. Religious education volunteers are special in large part because religious education work itself is special.

Let's take a closer look at each of these three fundamental underpinnings for the specialness of religious education activity.

Matthew's Gospel tells us that just before he was about to ascend into heaven, Jesus gathered together his apostles on a mountaintop (Mt 28:16-20). There he gave his final command to the original church leaders on

what he wanted his church to become then and forever. Scripture scholars call this final command to his apostles "The Great Commission."
Jesus' final command was simple and direct and summarized what he
wished the central mission of the church to be. In fact, Jesus gave only two
final commands to his church leaders. He wanted the church to baptize
(and by implication to conduct worship services), *and* he wanted the
church to do religious education. In other words, if the church baptizes
(and conducts worship services) and engages in religious education it is
doing all that is essential for the continuance of Jesus's mission on earth.

Since that day when Jesus gave The Great Commission, a host of
worthwhile and dynamic ministries have arisen in the long annals of the
church. Some of these apostolic works were born of a particular age and
died with the passing of that age, as for example the ministry of ran-
soming the captives from the Arabs in the Middle Ages. Other ministries
were born in a certain age and continue down to the present, such as visiting the sick at home or in a hospital. Notwithstanding, the two activities
which Jesus himself stated are central, necessary, and sufficient, remain
the same: baptism/worship and religious education. All other church
ministries, while very helpful and important, are nonetheless peripheral
to the essential mission of the church as judged by the standards set forth
by Jesus in Matthew 28:16-20.

As a general rule, the task of leading worship services belongs to the
clergy. This is especially true in the sacramental churches and most especially true in those sacramental churches which hold that only the clergy
by virtue of ordination share the eucharistic and redemptive power of
Jesus in a special way. So while the task of leading worship is recognized by most churches as belonging primarily to the clergy, the task of
religious education is one shared fully by the layperson. This is particularly true in our own time when so many clergy have unfortunately down-
played or even abandoned their central religious education obligations. In
today's churches, therefore, worship is conducted primarily by the clergy while religious education is conducted primarily by laypersons, including volunteers.

The second reason for the intense luminosity of religious education
within the galaxy of those church activities which are fully open to lay participation is that by engaging in religious education the layperson fol-
lows more closely the earthly lifework of Jesus than is the case with
other ministries. As I pointed out in my chapter in Joseph Marino's book
Biblical Themes in Religious Education, Jesus engaged in two principal
tasks while on earth. He was a redeemer and he was a religious educator.

The Bible clearly shows that Jesus was not principally a theologian, not principally a social worker, not principally a healer of the sick, not principally a commentator on the socioeconomic affairs of the day, and so forth. Of course Jesus did engage in all these activities, but they were not his central or main activities. Indeed the Bible shows that whenever Jesus did engage in these activities he did so almost exclusively to illustrate, expand upon, or enhance his two central tasks of redemption and religious education.

Some Christians like to go on pilgrimage to modern-day Israel in order to walk in the actual *physical* footsteps of Jesus, to walk where he walked. But it is not necessary to travel all the way to Israel to follow in Jesus's *ministerial* footsteps. By engaging in the same central mission that Jesus himself had, namely, that of religious education, laypersons can follow even more closely in the ministerial footsteps of Jesus than by visiting Israel. No other ministry which is fully open to laypersons allows us to follow in the central ministry of Jesus more than does religious education work.

Parenthetically, it should be noted that the Bible is not primarily a theological treatise, not primarily a social document, not primarily a historical record, or the like. The Bible does indeed contain all these elements, but first and foremost the Bible is a religious education document. The inspired authors of the books of the Bible saw both the scripture and themselves primarily in religious education terms. The apostle Paul put it this way: "All the ancient scriptures were written for our instruction" (Rom 15:4). Toward the end of the Ancient Period, Augustine wrote that the Spirit of God who spoke through the inspired biblical authors was unwilling to teach human beings those things which could not somehow be profitable for their salvation. In the Middle Ages, Thomas Aquinas held the same view: "The Spirit did not wish to tell us through the authors whom he inspired any other truth than that which is profitable for our salvation." In our own day, clergy of all Christian faith traditions preach the gospel primarily in a religious education way, namely as teaching persons how to live in a Godlike manner. So central was religious education to the apostle Paul's mission that he did not even baptize but rather devoted his efforts exclusively to religious education (1 Cor 1:17). The point of this paragraph is to suggest that because the Bible is primarily a religious education document, then Christians are particularly biblical when they do as the Bible does, namely, teach religion.

The third major reason why religious education stands head and shoulders above other ministries fully available for lay leadership is that the exercise of religious education requires a greater degree of competence from its practitioners than does virtually any other church ministry. This is true not only for professional religious educators but for volunteer religious educators as well. Let's explore this important point for a bit.

Religious education is the facilitation of desired learning outcomes in the learner. This definition reveals that religious education is both an art and a science. As an art, religious education requires that the teacher possess a wide range of practical skills necessary for insuring that the desired learning outcomes do in fact take place. These skills include a whole host of instructional strategies, methods, and techniques, most of which have to be mastered at least to a minimal degree by anyone who wishes to effectively teach religion, be that person a professional or a volunteer. Possession of these multiple instructional skills is not enough to be a successful religious educator. What is absolutely essential is that the religious educator be able to *enact* these skills competently with a here-and-now group of learners. The heart of this enactment is that the religious educator be able to continuously structure and restructure the four major ingredients present in every religious education event in such a way that the learner actually does learn what is supposed to be learned. These four major ingredients, by the way, are the teacher, the learner, the subject-matter content, and the facilitational environment.

The art of teaching is not free-floating; it is based on the science of teaching/learning. The practice of teaching, then, is the practice of a theory, in our case the theory of how to *teach* religion. Thus to be consistently effective, the volunteer religious educator has to know at least the rudiments of a workable theory of teaching/learning as well as the key laws and scientifically validated facts upon which this theory rests.

And the religious educator must also know the subject-matter content. A person just doesn't teach; a person must teach something, and that something is religion. It is crucial, and perhaps reassuring, to the volunteer that the subject-matter content of religious education is religion and not primarily theology. Of course theology often plays a role in the teaching of religion. But this is far different from equating theology with religion. The religious educator is a religious educator and not primarily a theological educator. As virtually every world-class theologian readily admits, religion consists in holistically living in a godly manner, while theology is an intellectual activity consisting in getting to know God and his ways better. Religion is living and doing, while theology is thinking.

Volunteerism in Religious Education Is a Very Serious Matter

So far this chapter has highlighted in a number of ways the fact that volunteerism in religious education is a very serious matter. Because of the sublimity of their work, religious education volunteers are obliged before God, before the church, before learners, and before themselves to take their divine calling with utmost seriousness. Religious education work is far different in its level of preparation and in its complexity of enactment than any other church ministry open fully to laypersons, ministries such as being a Lady of the Altar, doling out food to homeless persons at the church soup kitchen, visiting the sick, and the like.

It is a sad but well-known fact that many church officials fail to take religious education volunteerism with the great seriousness this exalted apostolate merits. Quite a few church officials seem to regard volunteers as a way of staffing the religious education program without having to pay for it. In other words, church officials like volunteers because they are free. One of the many downsides to this mentality is that since volunteers work for nothing or next to nothing, little in the way of genuinely adequate preservice or inservice training of religious education volunteers can be reasonably expected. Indeed, some religious education volunteers believe they are doing the local church a big favor by volunteering.

A second major disvaluation of religious education work by many church officials is the erroneous belief that anyone can teach religion and thus can be an effective volunteer. In this view, as long as a volunteer is a churchgoing Christian, he or she automatically possesses the instructional knowledge and skills necessary to be a successful religion teacher. Possibly the volunteer's automatic competence can be burnished a bit with an ever so brief smattering of preservice training, if time permits. These church officials, alas, are generally unaware of the overwhelming body of research which shows that teaching is a highly complex activity requiring a great deal of ongoing preservice and inservice training. Indeed, successful teaching is far more complex and more difficult than successful preaching. Personal piety does not exempt a person, even a churchgoing Christian person, from competence in the principles, theory, and procedures of effective teaching.

How many of the church officials described in the preceding paragraphs would entrust their own physical health or the physical well-being of their families to physicians who never went to medical school but who are lay volunteers with little or no training in the healing arts? Yet these selfsame church officials entrust the spiritual well-being of their congregations to volunteers who have little or no systematic ongoing training in the theory and practice of religion teaching. Is the care of the body of so much greater value than the care of the soul?

What can be done now and in the future to enable local churches to accord religious education volunteerism that supreme degree of seriousness which this exalted evangel rightly deserves? Correlatively, what can be done now and in the future to make the parish's religious education program as effective as possible because of the presence and the teaching activity of volunteers? These two pivotal questions will be addressed in the next section of this chapter.

The Key to Successful Religious Education Volunteerism

More than any other single factor, the quality and success of a religious education program depends on professionalism. But how does professionalism fit in with volunteerism? After all, volunteers are not professional religious educators and probably never will be. The chief point about professionalism is not that everyone working in the religious education program needs to be a professional. Rather, the key point is that *the program as a whole needs to be thoroughly professional* — a professional program. When the program is professional, everyone working in the program, full-time as well as volunteer, will become professional in that everyone will become an integral part of a competent, task-oriented enterprise which is professional to the core.

A professional religious education program is characterized by many major factors. Four of these factors are structure, partnership, growth, and dignity.

A professional religious education program is one whose structure is characterized by many interlocking elements and persons, all of which are regarded as important to attain the objectives of the program. The focus always is on how each element and each person singly and together can best work to attain the program's objectives in the most competent way possible. In a nonprofessional program, volunteers are concretely *apart* both from the structure as a whole and from professional religious educators within the structure — slogans and pious rhetoric from pastors notwithstanding. In a professional program, volunteers are concretely a *part* both of the overall structure and of the work of the professional religious educators within the structure. In a nonprofessional program, volunteers are outside the structure and thus typically are excluded from the meaningful determination of goals, objectives, parameters, and resources of the overall religious education program. In a professional program, volunteers are part of the structure and have an appropriate voice in the meaningful determination of the goals, objectives, parameters, and resources of the overall religious education program.

A professional religious education program is one in which there is full-fledged partnership among all the persons working in that program. Professionalism always means working together on a common task in a competent fashion to achieve a desired goal. Working together truly and competently necessitates partnership. This partnership does not mean that each partner performs the same task as the other partners, or has the same role or even an equal role. Rather, full-fledged partnership means that each person in the professional structure takes on that task best suited to his/her breadth and depth of natural abilities, training, and life experiences. Full-fledged partnership suggests, for example, that the professional religious educator not serve as a teacher aide, or that an untrained person who has just volunteered not be given an advanced religion class to teach.

A professional religious education program is one which directly promotes the professional growth of both volunteers and full-time workers. The structure of a professional program is such that the program contains within itself an ongoing series of first-class planned activities in which all religious educators, volunteers as well as full-time, not only (1) learn the principles and skills necessary to enhance the effectiveness of their present religious education tasks but also (2) learn those religious education skills which will enable the person to develop those competencies necessary for assuming increasingly advanced educational responsibilities within the structure.

Finally, a professional religious education program is one in which every religious educator, regardless of position or task, enjoys dignity. This dignity flows from the professional quality of the structure itself. When a religious education program is thoroughly professional, then every worker, full-time or volunteer, necessarily shares in the dignity which professionalism brings to every structure. All too often religious education volunteers have little or no dignity in the eyes of the pastor, the full-time religious education professionals, or even the congregation because these persons possess considerably less educational skills than does the professional religious educator. In any comparison between the full-time religious educator and the volunteer, the volunteer will almost always come out on the short end. When, however, a volunteer is a full-fledged member of a religious education structure which is professional, his/her competencies are not gauged on the basis of how they compare to those of the professional religious educator but on the basis of how these competencies contribute to the operation of the whole religious education program.

The Religious Educator Lattice

As the previous section of this chapter has demonstrated, professionalism is the most important single factor in contributing to the success of the religious education program. But how do volunteers, who by and large are nonprofessionals in religious education, fit into a religious education program which is thoroughly professional? The answer is the religious educator lattice.

As its name implies, a lattice is an overall framework. In a religious educator lattice, each major cluster of instructional tasks is placed in an ordered structural relationship with all the other major clusters. What results is an integrated network in which each instructional task has an intrinsic organic relationship to all the other clusters. Each cluster on the lattice is separate but related. The easiest way to understand what a lattice is and how it works is to form a picture in one's mind of a garden lattice or trellis. Because the religious education enterprise is task-oriented, each religious educator assumes a place in the trellis according to his/her competencies. The lattice described in this chapter refers only to the religious educator. There may be other lattices both in the religious education program and in the local church structure as a whole.

There are three main levels within a congregation's religious educator lattice. In descending order, these three levels are the professional religious educator, the paraprofessional religious educator, and the subprofessional religious educator. Volunteers typically assume roles and functions as paraprofessional religious educators or as subprofessional religious educators.

It is important to note that the word professional appears in the title of each of these three levels. This unambiguously suggests that each level is identified and demarked in terms of its place within the overall professional structure. Only when each and every level is viewed as an integral element of a professional structure can each person within that structure be an active appropriate partner who has dignity and competence. Only when each level within the structure is seen in terms of overall professionalism can each element play its proper role. In short, it is the professional structure which gives each person in each level that richness, dignity, and quality of task performance so necessary for successful religious education activity.

Teamwork and the religious educator lattice go hand in hand. The professional structure of the parish religious education program requires that full-time religious educators and volunteers work together coopera-

tively and reciprocally, each discharging appropriate tasks with competence and harmony. It is undeniably true that the professional religious educator is the key person in the lattice, the standard from which all other lattice levels are determined and the role into which all auxiliary roles flow.
It is also true that the primary task of the auxiliary religious educator is
to be just that, an auxiliary who help the professional religious educator
discharge his/her instructional role as successfully as possible. In every
team there is a leader and there are auxiliaries. In a true team, not everyone is the leader. This does not mean that the role of the leader is the
only role that counts and that the role of the auxiliaries is unimportant. On
the contrary, the work of properly trained auxiliaries is helpful and indeed
vital to the implementation of a first-class religious education program.
Hence volunteer religious educators should rightfully feel a great sense
of religious satisfaction and personal pride in the knowledge that their
activities are contributing significantly to the religious growth of those
learners with whom they come into direct or indirect contact. The volunteer should never feel that he/she is "only a volunteer" or "only a
helper." Few if any major health or religious organizations would be
where they are today if they did not have persons who functioned in an
auxiliary capacity. The same is true of virtually all businesses and indus-
tries. In the congregation's religious educator lattice, all persons, professionals and paraprofessionals alike, are all organically and structurally
members of the overall religious education team.

The Professional Religious Educator

The professional religious educator is the core, the mainstay, and the
touchstone of the parish or congregation religious education program.
He/she is the standard by which all other persons, responsibilities, and
tasks in the program are measured. In other words, the roles and functions
of every person in the professional religious education program are con-
ceptualized and deployed as a direct consequence of their relationship to
the roles and functions of the professional religious educator. The professional religious educator is not a volunteer. Rather, the professional religious educator is a well-trained and adequately paid full-time employee
of the local church devoting his/her time exclusively to religious education.

The professional religious educator is the individual primarily responsible for initiating, planning, enacting, and evaluating the religious instruction given to persons for whom he/she is responsible. One professional
religious educator might serve as the chief administrator of the overall pro-

gram, with other professional religious educators responsible for teaching religion to various kinds of persons in the parish.

The professional religious educator is one who has received preservice preparation from a university or seminary both in religious studies and in the theory and practice of teaching. This preservice preparation should minimally be equal to, and preferably superior to that received by public school teachers. Additionally, professional religious educators continue to engage in regular inservice experiences designed to further enhance their substantive knowledge and teaching skills. Such inservice experiences typically include receiving a Master of Arts degree in religious education, attendance at professional high-level workshops and conferences devoted to sharpening instructional competencies in various religious education areas, and the like.

Typically volunteers are part-time and unpaid — or paid only a token amount. Moreover, they usually lack the level of theoretical and practical training possessed by the professional religious educator. The only exception to this important rule occurs when public school teachers volunteer their services on a part-time basis. But even in such cases, these teachers often lack that level of training in substantive religious content to be on a par with the professional religious educator.

Where volunteers can be successful both in furthering the goals of the program and in meeting their own needs is by serving as paraprofessional religious educators or as subprofessional religious educators. Volunteers at both these lattice levels can be of signal assistance in making the overall parish religious education program a resounding success. Indeed, Carl Grant's review of the research indicates that by and large the use of paraprofessionals in public schools has improved the teaching/learning process and has exerted a positive impact on student achievement and attitudes. Grant's review of the research also found that professional public schoolteachers who were initially reluctant to work with paraprofessionals came to value their assistance and support after seeing firsthand how these paraprofessionals successfully helped to provide effective education to the students.

Very few volunteers possess the level of theoretical and practical training in both religious studies and in the art/science of teaching which the professional religious educator enjoys. Aware of their lack of adequate professional training, many otherwise capable parishioners often are reluctant to volunteer their services to the church's religious education program. What is wonderful about the paraprofessional and subprofessional levels in the overall religious educator lattice is that there is a place for everyone, a place in which all parishioners can utilize their own talents and experiences, a place in which all parishioners can feel comfortable knowing that they are giving the program those special gifts which they possess by virtue of their background, training, and experience, and a place which lets nonprofessional religious education personnel contribute significantly to the overall professional program.

The Paraprofessional Religious Educator

The paraprofessional religious educator is a person who assists the professional religious educator in the instructional efforts of the congregation's overall religious education program. Paraprofessional religious educators are instructional auxiliaries. These religious educators are paraprofessional in the sense that it is not their primary responsibility to plan, enact, innovate, or evaluate instructional activities on their own initiative or without direct supervision. Rather, paraprofessional religious educators take their direction from the professional religious educator as the local church endeavors to significantly extend the effectiveness of the learning process.

Paraprofessionals are auxiliaries to the professional religious educator. They are not substitutes for the professional religious educator. Except in dire straits when not enough professional religious educators can be found, paraprofessionals should not be expected to assume the major responsibilities of the professional religious educator.

There are four levels of paraprofessional religious educators. In descending order these four levels are teacher intern, teacher associate, teacher assistant, and teacher aide.

Teacher Intern. A teacher intern is a paraprofessional who provides high-level auxiliary teaching services to just one professional religious educator in the local church. The work of the teacher intern is directly or indirectly supervised and coordinated by the professional religious educator whom the teacher intern is helping.

Some illustrative functions of the teacher intern include cooperative planning with the teacher of the lesson, working to develop a learning environment which is highly educative, motivating learnings, working on teacher and learner committees, and conducting regular teaching activities. These regular teaching activities include leading group discussions, conducting role-playing lessons, directing problem-solving activities, providing individualized teaching, lecturing, leading learner symposia, initiating case studies, and using the project method.

Typically, the teacher intern is in the final stages of a religious education program or a general teacher education program at a local college or university, a program leading to a Bachelor's degree and certification as a professional teacher.

Teacher Associate. A teacher associate is a paraprofessional who provides intermediate-level auxiliary teaching services to one or a group of professional religious educators in the local church. The work of the teacher associate is directly or indirectly supervised and coordinated by the professional religious educator whom the teacher associate is helping.

Some illustrative functions of the teacher associate include helping the professional religious educator identify the needs and interests of the child/youth/adult learners, helping the professional religious educator identify the learner's intelligence level and level of religious achievement, helping the professional religious educator prepare teacher-made instructional materials both written and audiovisual, helping learners to study better, helping learners use worksheets and instructional kits, helping learners write their personal and religious journals, helping learners use educational games, telling stories to learners, and helping learners select appropriate books from the church library.

Recommended training for a teacher associate is a three-week course operated by the parish, diocese, or judicatory, with solid preparation in both the substantive content of religion and the theory and practice of teaching. Typically the teacher associate should have at least two years of college education. The teacher associate can be on a work-study basis while functioning as a teacher assistant.

Teacher Assistant. A teacher assistant is a paraprofessional who provides basic-level auxiliary teaching services to one or a group of professional religious educators in the local church. The work of the teacher assistant is directly or indirectly supervised and coordinated by the professional religious educator or group of educators whom the teacher assistant is helping.

Some illustrative functions of a teacher assistant include preparing and maintaining progress folders of the child/youth/adult learners, arranging for speakers to come in and talk with the learners, arranging for excursions to places or events of religious education interest, coordinating religious education award ceremonies, writing for free or inexpensive instructional materials from religious organizations and community agencies, decorating the learning environment (classroom, church building, church grounds, etc.) in a way which furthers religious education learnings, assembling realia and audiovisual materials of immediate or possible use in the religious instruction event, playing the piano or other musical instrument during the religious instruction event, helping learners become familiar with resources such as biblical concordances and atlases, arranging for the learners to participate in community service projects, and acting as liaisons between the religious education program on the one hand and pastor, parish counselors, and other parish workers on the other hand.

Recommended training for a teacher assistant consists in a one week course in which the prospective assistant learns about the goals and objectives of the parish religious education program, the general inner workings of the parish, the role and function of the professional religious educator, and also those duties which a teacher assistant is expected to perform. Typically the teacher assistant should have a year of college education. The teacher assistant can also be on a work-study basis while functioning as a teacher aide.

Teacher Aide. A teacher aide is a paraprofessional who provides basic nonteaching services to one or to a group of professional religious educators in the local church.

Some illustrative functions of a teacher aide include providing the professional religious educator with basic clerical assistance such as instructionally related record keeping, basic technical help such as typewriting and duplicating relevant instructional materials, and performing basic housekeeping tasks such as assuring that the lighting, temperature, seating, and the like, are all in order prior to the enactment of the religious instruction event.

Recommended training for a teacher aide consists in a three-day preparation period in which the prospective aide learns the rudimentary workings of the parish, finds out the basic goals and objectives of the religious education program, gets to know the role and functions of the professional religious educator, finds out the location and operation of instructionally related machines, and the like. Typically the teacher aide should have a high school diploma or the equivalent.

The Subprofessional Religious Educator

The subprofessional religious educator is a person who provides basic support services to the religious education program in the local church. The work of the subprofessional religious educator is generally not supervised by the professional religious educator but rather by other leaders in the local church.

Some illustrative functions of the subprofessional religious educator include driving a bus or van and preparing meals for consumption on the regular religious instruction site or on an excursion.

Recommended training for a subprofessional religious educator is a two-day orientation about the location and use of the busses or the kitchen and the like, plus some rudimentary information on the fundamental goals and structure of the parish's religious education program. During this orientation information should also be given about the way in which the subprofessional's work fits in and supports the program. Typically the sub-professional should have adequate training in the field of his/her volunteer work, such as a chauffeur's license and driving experience in the case of a bus driver.

The subprofessional is an integral and organic part of the parish's religious education team. The conversation which the bus driver or a van driver has with the child/youth/adult passengers, the way in which the driver decorates the bus or van with religious materials, the songs the driver elects to play in the vehicle's cassette system — all have a decidedly religious education effect. The same is true for the work of the other subprofessionals. In a lattice every person plays a decidedly helpful role in achieving the overall goal. In a lattice, all roles intersect and interact in a certain sense, thus improving the effectiveness of every unit within the lattice.

Ladder and Lattice

The levels and sublevels of the religious educator lattice suggest that this lattice can also serve as a ladder. The roles within the religious education lattice are horizontal to one another in terms of the harmonious cooperative interaction in the total religious education enterprise. But these roles are also vertical in the sense that each role partakes to a greater or lesser extent in the work of the professional religious educator. Thus each role entails a different vertical level of functioning and requires a different vertical level of training. This is why the religous educator lattice can also serve as a religious educator ladder for those volunteers wishing to use the lattice as a ladder.

There are doubtless many volunteers who would prefer to remain in their present place on the ladder as subprofessionals, as teacher aides, as teacher assistants, and so on. But there are doubtless other volunteers who might well wish to assume increasingly greater religious education responsibilities and rise up the ladder. One of the signal advantages of the religious educator lattice is that it offers both volunteers and the overall program an inbuilt orderly structure whereby volunteers can gain that training and experience to move up the ladder.

Religious Educator Lattice

Title	Illustrative Functions	Training

LEVEL I: PROFESSIONAL RELIGIOUS EDUCATOR

Title	Illustrative Functions	Training
Professional Religious Educator	Plans, enacts, and evaluates religious instruction activities.	B.A. degree in religious education or in general education. Preferably M.A. in religious education plus relevant inservice participation in workshops, conferences, etc.

LEVEL II: PARAPROFESSIONAL RELIGIOUS EDUCATOR

Title	Illustrative Functions	Training
Teacher Intern	Plans, enacts, and evaluates religious instruction activities under the direct immediate supervision of the professional religious educator.	Final stages of B.A. program in religious education or general education.
Teacher Associate	Helps professional religious educator to prepare instructional materials, to identify learner needs and interests; helps learners to use worksheets, write journals, and study better.	Two years of college plus four week initial parish preparation program in religious education, with later participation in workshops and conventions.
Teacher Assistant	Preparing and maintaining program folders on learners, arranging educational excursions, writing for instructional materials, help learners become familiar with educational resources, arranging for participation in community service.	One year of college plus two week initial parish preparation program in religious education with later participation in workshops and conventions.
Teacher Aide	Record keeping and other clerical work, typewriting, reproducing and duplicating instructional materials, regulating lighting and temperature.	High school diploma plus three day initial preparation program in religious education.

LEVEL III: SUBPROFESSIONAL RELIGIOUS EDUCATOR

Title	Illustrative Functions	Training
Collateral Religious Education	Bus or van driver, food preparer.	Training and experience in field of subprofessional work, plus one day initial preparation in parish program in religious education.

Three Concluding Points

Training

One of the features of the lattice model is its emphasis on preservice and inservice training. The importance of adequate training cannot be overestimated in religious education, or in any kind of education for that matter. Not surprisingly, the overwhelming body of research studies clearly shows that trained teachers are consistently more successful than untrained teachers. The lattice model provides a matrix in which each volunteer takes on that religious education task for which he/she has been adequately trained. The lattice model also supplies a framework in which each volunteer can deepen his/her competencies at the level at which he/she is serving. And finally, the lattice model offers a structure in which each person can be trained within the structure to undertake increasingly higher levels of religious education activity.

Thinking, Feeling, and Acting Educationally

In each of its parts as well as in its entirety, the lattice model is thrusted toward enabling the volunteer to approach his/her religious education task from an educational rather than from a noneducational perspective. Preservice and inservice training, together with active participation in religious education endeavor, are all designed to help the volunteer think, feel, and act educationally when discharging his/her religious education functions. A research study conducted by William McCready speaks eloquently to this point. McCready found that persons who worked in Catholic CCD (Sunday school) programs saw themselves either as educators or as ministers. Those teachers who identified their work as ministry tended to have unclear goals and unformulated objectives about their religious instruction work. These individuals also tended to minimize or even disparage the importance of working hard to improve their teaching skills. In contrast, those teachers who identified their work as education tended to have clear goals and well-formulated objectives about their religious instruction work. These persons also tended to emphasize the importance of working hard to improve their teaching skills. The results of McCready's study are germane to all religious educators, volunteers and professionals alike, since the relevant research studies indicate that clarity of goals, precision of objectives, and unremitting attention to the improvement of teaching skills are all correlated highly with teaching success.

Thinking, feeling, and acting educationally means thinking, feeling, and acting in such a way as to be oriented toward facilitating desired learning outcomes in others. This orientation, so necessary for successful religious instruction, is one way which is learned. It is not inborn. The structure and enactment of the lattice model is such that it organically enables the volunteer to consistently and habitually think, feel, and act in an educational fashion. The lattice, then, is a powerful and effective educator of volunteers in and of itself.

Idealism

Some local church leaders and religious education officials might say that the lattice model is idealistic and therefore impractical. Quite the opposite is the case. The lattice model is extremely practical because it ensures that the parish religious education program will work to maximum capacity. The lattice model is also extremely practical because it ensures that the congregation's religious education program will continually regenerate and improve itself from within.

The lattice model will work because it is intrinsically professional. Professionalism is necessary if the parish religious education activities are to be competent and successful. Without professionalism the religious education program is a hit-or-miss affair.

The lattice model will work because it guarantees that each religious educator at every level of the lattice will be trained to perform the functions required of that level. If the parish religious education program is to be essential, it is essential that it has personnel adequately trained to do the job they are supposed to do.

The lattice model will work because it provides clarity of role and functions with the entire religious education program. This clarity of role and functions enables each person within the lattice to have realistic expectations of exactly what he/she is supposed to do and not to do. And this clarity of role and functions enables the work of each person within the lattice to mesh harmoniously with the work of all other persons within the program, thus avoiding overlaps, duplications, and tasks not done.

Finally the lattice model will work because it supplies an inbuilt structure which enables a congregation's religious education program to improve itself by virtue of the ongoing structure itself. The lattice model takes the energy used in providing first-rate religious instruction to learners of all ages and uses this selfsame energy to continuously upgrade and improve all aspects of the program. In other words, the energy deployed by all members in the lattice not only results in high-quality religion teaching but also in program renewal. Not only is a place of dignity and competence provided by the lattice to persons of virtually every background, but also the structure of the lattice is such that persons at every level can move to the next higher level. Hence the lattice model enables the religious education program to regenerate itself from within, out of its own energies. This dynamic force for the inbuilt improvement of persons and program makes the lattice model an ideal one for churches of every size from the smallest to the largest. Thanks to the lattice, small churches are able to homegrow their own cadre of appropriately trained volunteers. Large churches, for their part, can maximize the efforts of volunteers through the lattice model.

Without vision, without the idealism which vision engenders, we all perish — church and religious education program alike (Prv 29:18). Thus for all Christians idealism is an extremely practical matter. Even more, idealism is a Christian imperative. If Jesus could tell his followers that they should be perfect just as their heavenly Father is perfect (Mt 5:48), is it likely that he would tell religious educators that they and their programs should strive for less than perfection? The religious education program will surely never be perfect, but unless it idealistically strives to be perfect it will never be true to the call of Jesus. From the Christian perspective, idealism, backed up by competence, is the ultimate practicality.

As was shown at the beginning of this chapter, religious education stands at the very center of the church and its many diverse ministries. Consequently, idealism and excellence are especially urgent guideposts and touchstones for the religious education program and for all those who work in it. If the parish religious education program does not model excellence in its structure and its personnel, how can the church expect that it will teach the Christian life successfully?

The remainder of this book will show how the church can build and maintain a truly successful religious education volunteer program. This book will thus show how all volunteers can be empowered to do their best to fulfill The Great Commission which Jesus gave to the church and to each religious education volunteer.

For Further Reading

Bowman, Garda, and Gordon Klopf. *New Careers and Roles in the American Schools*. New York: Bank Street College of Education, 1968.

Brotherman, Mary Lou, and Mary Ann Johnson. *Teacher Aide Handbook*. Danville, Ill.: Interstate, 1971.

DaSilva, Benjamin, and Richard D. Lucas. *Practical School Volunteer and Teacher-Aide Programs*. West Nyack, N.Y.: Parker, 1974.

Gage, N. L. *The Scientific Base of the Art of Teaching*. New York: Teachers College Press, 1978.

Grant, Carl, ed. *Preparing for Reflective Teaching*. Boston: Allyn & Bacon.

Houston, W. Robert, ed. *Handbook of Research on Teacher Education*. New York: Macmillan, 1990.

Lee, James Michael. "Religious Education and the Bible." In *Biblical Themes in Religious Education*, ed. Joseph S. Marino, pp. 1-61. Birmingham, Ala.: Religious Education Press, 1983.

Lee, James Michael, ed. *The Spirituality of the Religious Educator*. Birmingham, Ala.: Religious Education Press, 1985.

Mark, Jorie Lester. *Paraprofessionals in Education*. New York: Bank Street College of Education, 1975.

Wittrock, Merlin, ed. *Handbook of Research on Teaching*, 3rd ed. New York: Macmillan, 1968.

Part II

Planning for Religious
Education Volunteers

Chapter Five

What Needs Can Volunteers Meet?

At first glance this question appears to be the same one we considered in chapter three. However, there we considered the very open question of what tasks volunteers can, in general, perform in the church. Here we want to narrow our focus to meeting needs through religious education. What religious education needs can volunteers meet?

Paul Ilsley and John Niemi suggest five different categories of volunteerism, each of which can be reflected in different aspects of religious education:

1. *Advisors*. This would include members of the religious education committee and possibly subcommittees. Fund raisers and evaluators also might be included here.

2. *Administrators/clerical people*. The religious education director and assistants would be included here, as would clerks, typists, and other clerical support.

3. *Instruction-related personnel*. Specialists in developing and using educational materials, teachers, teachers' assistants, and others directly involved in teaching fit here.

4. *Supportive services*. Here we find those involved in transportation (e.g., driving church buses), child care workers, those who prepare snacks, custodians, and the like.

5. *Specialty positions*. Artists, counselors, researchers, those involved in public relations, and other specialists fall within this category. Perhaps some of these people could be itinerant, serving more than one religious organization in their volunteer efforts.

Needs vary from situation to situation. We cannot expect the religious education needs of a small, rural church of fifty to be the same as a large urban church of two thousand. Likewise a parachurch organization is likely to have different needs from a church. The key, then, is to determine what needs exist, and prioritize those needs so they can be met by volunteers.

Surveys and Questionaires

A needs analysis is a procedure that can be used to determine religious education needs and what priority each need should be given. In the typical religious education situation this can be accomplished either by a written survey or systematic interviews. The context of religious education determines who should be surveyed. [Note: the needs of the *surrounding* community will be considered in chapter six.]

For example, surveys are often given in a church to determine people's opinions of what needs have not been fully addressed (see James Engel's work). The survey consists of written questions about the individual's personal needs and whether they are fulfilled or not. To illustrate, a survey might include questions such as:

I am satisfied with what the church is now accomplishing
_____ true _____ false _____ not sure

I feel a real lack in my life that I wish the church would address
_____ true _____ false _____ not sure

I would like to participate in the following ministry not currently offered by the church:
_____ small Bible study groups
_____ weekday children's club
_____ camping with teens
_____ other_____

The above questions are closed-ended and as a result are easy to tabulate. Unfortunately they may not address all the options available or they may not concentrate upon the most important issues. Adding the category "other" and a blank or two for people to fill in other options helps some, at least when those filling them out have a knowledge of the many possibilities. While a pastor or religious education director may be able to list many possibilities, it may be better for the religious education committee or another select group to brainstorm possibilities to be listed on the survey.

Another survey method is simply to leave blanks next to questions similar to the above:

The areas where this church is doing well are:_____
The areas where this church could do better are:_____
I would like to participate in the following areas of ministry:

_____

This approach allows for more possibilities than the previous approach but is limited by the creativity of the person filling out the questionaire. One pastor who recognized the religious education responsibilities of pulpit ministry used such an approach with a simple question, "I wish the pastor would preach a sermon on _____." The result was the development of an entire series of messages on the family.

It is possible to combine these two kinds of questionnaires in a single survey. It is also possible to survey a few people with the blanks to find most of the possibilities, then survey the whole church with a fixed option questionaire.

Instead of using questionaires, interviews also can be a good approach to finding the needs of the church. Instead of filling out a survey on paper, one or more people in the church talk personally to church attenders or members. This approach takes more time and effort, although telephone calls instead of meeting personally may speed up the process. Generally churches that go with the interview approach do not survey the whole church, because of the time required, but instead select some part of the church or group. The target group could be teenagers, the elderly, singles, recent newcomers, and so on. While the interviewer should prepare a number of questions in advance, he or she needs to encourage persons interviewed to discuss their answers in detail. For example, the interviewer might say, "What do you wish this church was doing that it is not at present?" "What would that involve?" "Are there others who have such an interest? Would you mind sharing with me their names?" "What experience have you had in that area?" and so on.

As a result of using questionaires or interviews, the religious educator may get a better idea of what the church genuinely needs in the area of religious education. Of course this approach is generally limited to members' or attenders' opinions of what is needed. This may need to be supplemented with the opinions of the denomination or church leaders. Either the same or a separate survey can also elicit the names of prospective volunteers (recruiting will be considered in detail in chapters eight through eleven).

Matching Talents to Needs

Once one has acquired the names of potential volunteers, matching abilities to needs is the next logical step. Yet these do not always match well; the abilities present may not fit into the existing program, while the most urgent needs may not be met because of lack of qualified people (or lack of *willing* qualified people).

If the difficulty is that no potential volunteers are available, the administrator must face the question of whether the program is worth having. As is mentioned several times in this book, the temptation is always present to try to fit the most available people into the most pressing need. But this will almost inevitably contribute to poor morale and burnout. Instead, as George Barna has pointed out, we must ask if a program can be viable if qualified people are unavailable to implement it. Clearly such a program cannot be done in a superior manner, and thus mediocrity is the result. The answer may be to look for other religious education tasks that can be done well, at the appropriate level of the religious education lattice (see chapter four).

On the other hand, the presence of people with talents that do not fit the present program may suggest that new programs need to be considered. Using a survey, hidden talents and interests may be uncovered that are common to several individuals. Some would suggest that this indicates the workings of providence; incidental gatherings of those with common abilities may indicate God's direction. Regardless of how one theologically analyzes such a situation, it is important to help individuals actualize their potential through volunteerism. If the present religious organization is unable to accomplish this and is unwilling to develop new programs, it is incumbent upon the leadership to direct these talented individuals to other organizations or churches where their talents can be used. While this might appear far-fetched, Barna notes that churches that are spiritually and numerically growing are the most likely to redirect such potential volunteers to other organizations that can maximally use their talents.

Religious education volunteer work must not be considered static and unchanging. Even in the Bible, people designated "table waiters" in the book of Acts actually did missionary and other evangelistic work. A successful volunteer program allows a degree of flexibility, so that to some extent a position can be customized to the individual volunteer. We will consider the topic of volunteer roles in greater detail in chapter seven.

Pyramid of Leadership

Ilsley and Niemi cite evidence for a pyramid of leadership. At the top of the pyramid are the careerists, or what James Michael Lee (chapter four) calls "professionals." This is the smallest group in the church, but they have the greatest responsibility and should have the greatest amount of preparation. The part-time people, or "paraprofessionals" in the Lee approach, are more numerous than the first category but have less responsibility and less preparation. A third category is what Lee calls the "sub-professionals," who have the least responsibility and least amount of preparation.

Clearly when one examines the pyramid of leadership (or Lee's lattice), the importance of volunteers is underscored. Without a large number of volunteers, most churches could not have a religious education program.

Delegating

How does responsibility become diffused within an organization? Generally tasks and responsibilities move down the pyramid through delegating. In church and parachurch settings the church board, pastor or priest, or other church authority delegates to the director of religious education or an equivalent position. Eventually tasks and responsibilities are delegated to the individual volunteer.

Good delegating is more than just telling others what to do and expecting them to perform the assigned tasks. The American Society for Training and Development offers seven tips for effective delegating:

1. It is important to carefully *choose the right volunteer* for the right task. As a result, volunteers will not be overwhelmed with the task, but instead develop with the job.

2. *Communicate specifications* for the task. The volunteer should know as many details as possible, from beginning to end, of what the job requires.

3. *Volunteers need to sense some control.* Those at the upper levels of the religious education lattice may ultimately be responsible for the outcomes, but volunteers also should have authority. Those in charge can let volunteers make some decisions by releasing some control. The volunteer takes a measure of responsibility and authority for the specific task, while the ultimate responsibility for religious education resides in those at upper levels of the lattice. The ASTD emphasizes that managers must be careful that volunteers not be allowed to use "reverse delegation," redelegating back to program directors.

4. *Checkpoints* are needed. There must be an evaluation process by which directors receive feedback to be sure the task is being accomplished and deadlines met. This is formative evaluation (see chapter fourteen).

5. As much as possible, *delegate an entire task*. Satisfaction and pride are maximal when a volunteer accomplishes an entire task rather than just fragmented parts of the task. Yet it is important that the volunteer not be overwhelmed with the task. In religious education, a teacher's assistant might be considered an entire task — when adequately defined in a job description — even though the person is obviously assisting the principal teacher.

6. *Encouragement* is crucial. Confidence toward the volunteer should be expressed concretely through praise, while criticism must be directed toward the job, not the worker.

7. Summative *evaluation* should be provided. At the conclusion of the task or time-period, a final assessment will indicate areas needing improvement. Formative evaluation is also crucial, as will be described in detail later.

These seven guidelines clearly indicate that delegating cannot be separated from the broader volunteer process — from beginning to end, delegating is central to volunteerism. The above tips indicate that the *way* delegating occurs will make or break religious education volunteer programs. The administrator who fails either to delegate completely enough, or — conversely— fails to follow up sufficiently is likely to have less than optimal results. Volunteers may be dissatisfied and leave, or the religious education task will not be accomplished with high quality.

Some directors of religion education are more reluctant to delegate to volunteers than others. Why might this be the case? It is probably a matter of trust. Developmental psychologist Erik Erikson believes that people who are generally more trusting were raised in home environments where others met their needs consistently. Thus the embryonic ability to trust in infancy and toddlerhood is perhaps tied in with the ability to trust throughout life. In addition, other experiences subsequent to childhood affect the degree to which one can trust others. Negative past experiences with untrustworthy religious education volunteers may create a greater hesitancy to delegate in the future.

Sometimes the hesitancy to delegate may be related to the perception of status differences. Delegating may be perceived as the conveyance of power, and power-oriented administrators may be unwilling to share power with those considered to be of lower status. Status differences between professional religious educators and religious education volunteers are probably inevitable, but a genuine sense of community and ownership of the program (and thus motivation to perform) comes from an egalitarian sharing of power. Perhaps some directors of religious education volunteer programs believe that delegating only conveys power, not responsibility. In these cases, it is crucial to emphasize to religious education volunteers that both power and authority are to be delegated, even though — as noted previously — overall responsibility continues to reside in the administrator.

For Further Reading

Barna, George. *User-Friendly Churches*. Glendale, Calif.: Regal, 1991.

Engel, James. "Conducting a Needs Analysis." In *Handbook of Youth Ministry*, ed. Donald Ratcliff, pp. 275-295. Birmingham, Ala.: Religious Education Press, 1991.

Ilsley, Paul, and John Niemi. *Recruiting and Training Volunteers*. New York: McGraw-Hill, 1981.

The Atlanta Journal, 19 August 1991, p. E8. "Management experts offer tips on delegating more effectively." Reprinted from *The Washington Post*.

For a detailed summary of Erik Erikson's theory and its applications to religious education, see Paul Meier, et al., Introduction to Psychology and Counseling, *2nd ed. Grand Rapids, Mich.: Baker, 1991. This book also includes many other applications to religious education.*

Chapter Six

Forming the Goals of the Volunteer Program

A goal never set is never reached. It is a sad commentary on churches that too often they go from week to week, and even year to year, without a clear plan for the future. Groups often go nowhere because no one has planned anywhere for them to go. But where do goals come from? Ideally they should come from the needs people have in a community. Need-driven goals are those that are most likely to be met and to have a significant impact upon others.

Goals Come from Needs

How can a religious organization discover the needs in a community? Paul Maves, in his book on volunteerism, suggests six ways:

1. *Develop a group* of concerned people who represent the local community, and let them share what they believe to be the needs in the area. This group may not always include community leaders, although they sometimes can contribute. Talking with people "on the other side of the tracks" and those easily ignored by others may help you find the most desperate concerns. Applied to religious education, this committee would probably include public school educators who are interested in religious education and perhaps religious leaders from minority groups. A variety of people from one's constituency is also desirable.

2. *Keep an open ear* to those who are hurting. Sometimes people are hesitant to share their needs because they fear rejection or may become embarrassed. An openness to the cries of these needy people, sometimes cries that cannot be verbally uttered (such as the cry of the abused child), communicates a sense of caring and concern. Stories in local newspapers may be one way to hear of such needs. In the religious education context,

it is important to have some means of obtaining input from those in the congregation that need help. Religious educators need to be able to reach out to individuals such as the sick and dying with religious education appropriate to their situation.

3. *Systematically survey* the community. Demographic studies, census data, university research projects, planning commissions, and other sources of statistical information can be helpful if the statistics are read compassionately. Religious education efforts should likewise respond to such data, particularly data related to religious thinking, attitudes, and behavior. Surveying the church for people's understanding of religious concepts and values might be a viable approach. Using sources of relevant research, such as Kenneth Hyde's *Religion in Childhood and Adolescence* for children and youth ministry, can also help target needs (for example he documents evidence for the decline in religious belief among young adolescents, an area that needs to be specifically addressed by religious educators). A needs analysis, as described in chapter five, might be considered.

4. *Remain open* to new areas of need and ways of meeting needs. Sometimes members of religious groups really want to help others but are unable to formulate a reasonable, workable plan to accomplish that help. Observing what others have attempted and whether those ideas have succeeded or failed can help. This suggests that religious educators in a given community should meet with their counterparts from other organizations. Dialogue and discussion about what is occurring and previous attempts can help all involved avoid repetition of errors and perhaps even coordinate ongoing efforts.

5. *Develop a pilot program.* A brief experiment may help test how genuine a need is and how likely a program is to meet that need. Even if the pilot program does not work, it may provide helpful information about alternative possible programs or more appropriate timing of interventions. For example, the religious education department of a church might try a small, pilot program of teaching biblical concepts to minority children in a nearby community center. In the process they may discover that using minority teachers would be more effective in such an outreach, or that the effort would be more successful if done in a cooperating minority church. Another example would be a released time effort directed towards only the children in a particular church could be a pilot project for a broader program reaching children in public schools generally.

6. *Prioritize* needs. The above approaches will probably unearth a wide variety of needs, all of which cannot be met by any single group. The

degree of urgency and the available resources must be taken into account to meet needs. There are many different approaches religious education volunteer efforts can take, as seen in chapter five, and thus those that are most needed and can be done with the highest quality should take priority.

Needs must be related to what members of the local church or religious organization are willing to do. While religious people may be hesitant or unwilling to minister to some urgent areas of need, there may be other areas of need that they will be willing to become involved with. One must listen not only to the needy but also to one's constituency. Of course, one area of need may be to help change the concerns of one's constituency to meet the most urgent needs.

Setting Goals

Once the needs of the group or the targeted community have been discovered, the goals of the religious education program can be developed. Goals directly relate to meeting needs. Indeed, meeting those needs constitutes the goals to be set.

Setting goals must be an orderly, sequential process. In other words, you cannot expect to meet people's needs all at once, but instead one needs to set reasonable, sensible sub-goals. After sub-goals have been set, they may have to be changed because the step is still too large to be met at one time.

Goal setting is often addressed in religious education literature by a concern for terminal objectives, implementing objectives, and so on. Generally the emphasis is upon setting goals that involve observable actions of the learner or at least measurable activities.

To illustrate, a church may find that a number of people would like to meet together to discuss how the Bible relates to everyday life. A small group might be formed that meets in one member's home. The goal of using the Bible in a relevant manner can be broken down into the subgoals of:

1. Reading a particular Bible passage
2. Interpreting that Bible passage accurately
3. Extracting one or more key principles from that Bible passage
4. Applying those principles to the lives of individuals in the group

Theoretically it might be possible for the leader to do the first three steps alone, as generally occurs in a sermon, but group discussion at each step makes it likely that members will be more involved, as well as learn the overall process involved. Teaching each step, through explanation, discussion, examples, and trial-and-error by participants, makes it more likely that each participant will be able to master the entire process. While learning the skill of applying the Bible is the goal in this example, it should be noted that meeting together to make applications is another legitimate goal, in which the group activity, not skills to be learned, would be the objective.

Mission Statement and Philosophy

Ilsley and Niemi emphasize the different kinds of goals found in volunteer organizations. The most broad goal is called the "mission statement." Parachurch organizations are more likely to have such a statement than a local church, but all religious organizations need to think carefully about what they are attempting to accomplish and then reflect this in a mission statement.

Maves believes that the best place to form a statement of mission is during conferences which are specifically intended to make plans for the religious organization's future. Questions need to be asked during the conference, such as, "What is the purpose of this organization?" "How can this congregation help fulfill God's plan?" "How can we love God and our neighbor concretely in this community?" and even "What neighbor does God want us to minister to?"

The mission statement provides a point of reference for worship services, prayer, Bible study, singing of hymns, sermons, and reflections on church history. While vague generalizations rarely motivate people, a succinct statement of purpose and mission gives direction than can help motivate.

Church researcher George Barna notes that spiritually healthy and numerically growing churches tend to have pastors who describe the mission of the church regularly, and the congregation is very aware of the mission of the church. The mission is more than just religious platitudes but rather a clear view of where the church is to move. The mission statement does not include everything spiritual but rather specifies those areas that a particular church or religious organization will concentrate its efforts. Fundamental to the mission statement is a workable plan which the church leaders continually hold out as the direction for the church.

Examples of mission statements include, "Our church will reach those in the community that are not currently a part of another church by providing distinctive ministry focusing on worship and praise." Another example might be, "Relational ministry is the purpose of Trinity Church, which emphasizes personal interaction with others primarily in small groups and secondarily within a large congregation." A third example could be, "Biblical teaching and preaching, with an emphasis upon using concepts in everyday life, is the basic goal of this church." Parachurch organizations are likely to have an even more targeted mission statement, such as, "This day camp will provide physical, social, and spiritual nurture for children from impoverished families."

Closely related to the mission statement is the operating philosophy of education for the religious organization. This philosophy should have succinct statements about the role of religious education, and the religious education committee should expand that philosophy in detail. An example of a philosophy statement (not a complete philosophy) might be: "The religious education of children will be a priority, including the nurture of faith, the knowledge of the Bible, and the application of religious truths by children." Another example could be, "Our goal is ministry to single adults, both Christian and non-Christian, through recreational, social, and spiritual activities." A comprehensive philosophy of education involves several such statements, all of which fall within the framework of the mission statement.

Long- and Short-Term Goals

After a mission statement has been developed for the church and a comprehensive philosophy of education created by the religious education committee (or its equivalents in parachurch groups), long-term goals should be articulated. What specific classes or groupings can be developed (or continued) that directly relate to the operating philosophy? Again, this must be related constantly to the needs that were determined in the needs analysis (chapter five and earlier in this chapter). In a sense the operating philosophy provides the general direction of the long-term objectives, while the needs analysis indicates the more specific content of those objectives. Long-term objectives may need to be revised periodically to determine if they are still needed or if change is required. New, supplementary goals may be required.

To illustrate a long-term goal related to the above philosophy statement, one might suggest that "children will have a working knowledge of the location of books of the Bible." This is a goal that will take several weeks to accomplish, and it directly relates to the phrase "knowledge of the Bible" in the philosophy statement.

In forming the goals of the religious education endeavor, ancillary services must not be overlooked. For example, if it is determined that a special class is needed for new parents, babysitting for babies and young children will probably be needed. Books and supplies may need to be provided. Some ancillary services may be performed by subprofessionals, while others may require the work of paraprofessionals.

Long-term goals are accomplished through the developing and use of objectives. These are more short-term, specific, and precise statements of what should be done by the student. They describe observable, measurable behavior. For example a short-term goal related to the earlier examples would be "third grade children will be able to locate the book of Daniel within thirty seconds, given a Bible." This statement might be accomplished in a single session of the group. Also note that the thirty seconds is a measurement, while locating the book is an observable behavior.

The best-known proponent of performance objectives, Robert Mager, recommends that objectives be developed using three guidelines. First, the desired behavior needs to be stated in measurable and usually observable terms. Second, the circumstances and conditions under which the behavior occurs is defined. Third, the level or degree of precision required is specified. As a result of meeting these three criteria the outcomes desired will be explicit for the learner and teacher alike.

Developing goals and objectives can be a time-consuming and difficult process, although it is well worth the effort. Consult Starks and Ratcliff for a more detailed explanation of the process.

Myths and Fears

Ilsley and Niemi point out that reaching the goals of the volunteer program can be undermined by certain fears and myths. These are most likely to be held by professionals and perhaps paraprofessionals on the church staff.

First there is the fear that volunteers will take the place of professionals. Church leaders may wonder if the presence of lay Bible study leaders, as in the previous example, might decrease the need for an assistant pastor or minister of education. Generally, however, an increased number of volunteers creates a need for more professionals, not fewer. Lay leaders must be trained initially and given regular inservice instruction. If there is any turnover (which is likely) the initial training must be repeated.

Sometimes church leaders may feel volunteers have poor motives for involvement. Volunteers may be perceived as crusaders, ego-oriented, or do-gooders. Perhaps they get involved to overcome guilt or to meet their own needs, rather than having concern for the religious education needs of others. Certainly there can be a wide variety of motives for volunteer efforts, and Em Griffin has suggested that such a variety is a good thing. While motivation is important, just as important (some would say more important) is that the task is being accomplished. If the best possible religious education is taking place because of the involvement of volunteers, should we complain about less than ideal motives?

Do volunteers feel their tasks must be continually exciting and challenging? While professionals in the church may believe this is the case, many volunteers are more realistic about their tasks. However, it is a good idea for those who prepare volunteers to be sure they understand that there are routine aspects of the job at hand that are less than exciting sometimes.

Some church leaders feel that volunteers lack sufficient commitment to the task. George Barna's research of the church indicates that briefer commitment to a specific volunteer task in the church is likely in the years ahead. Rather than insisting upon a one year commitment to teaching a Sunday school or catechism class, you may be able to get more people involved by asking for three month commitments. Recommitments may be more likely if a short term is requested initially. It is simply unrealistic to insist upon long-term commitments from most volunteers (see chapter sixteen). But this does not mean volunteers have no place in the church, it simply means we may need to have a regular, ongoing recruitment and training program in which we expect and plan for many more people being involved for shorter spans of time. As Ilsley and Niemi point out, a constant flow of volunteers both in and out of service can revitalize the organization.

Another myth is that volunteers can be difficult to manage. While this can certainly be the case, it does not constitute an impossible problem. As will be considered later in this book, there is a place for reprimanding or even terminating volunteers. On the other hand, evaluating the work of the volunteer is a crucial aspect of supervising volunteers and participants worth having in a religious education program will probably welcome such evaluation.

Finally, some may believe that volunteers are a threat to loyalty. They may find out too much about the organization and stir up dissatisfaction in the church or parachurch group. Quite the opposite appears to be the case; most volunteers become strong advocates of the religious group. Involvement in the group is strongly related to wanting to help the group. In addition, volunteers can give valuable insights and encourage the open understanding of both strengths and weaknesses of the religious education program.

In sum, the myths and fears about volunteers are exaggerated. These must not be allowed to block the meeting of goals of the volunteer program.

For Further Reading

Barna, George. *User-Friendly Churches*. Ventura, Calif.: Regal, 1991.

Griffin, Em. *Getting Together*. Downers Grove, Ill.: InterVarsity, 1984.

Hyde, Kenneth. *Religion in Childhood and Adolescence*. Birmingham, Ala.: Religious Education Press, 1990.

Ilsley, Paul, and John Niemi. *Recruiting and Training Volunteers*. New York: McGraw-Hill, 1981.

Mager, Robert. *Preparing Instructional Objectives*. Palo Alto, Calif.: Fearon, 1962.

Maves, Paul. *Older Volunteers in Church and Community*. Valley Forge, Pa.: Judson, 1981.

Starks, David, and Donald Ratcliff. "Planning, Evaluation, and Research." In *Handbook of Preschool Religious Education*, ed. Donald Ratcliff, pp. 270-287. Birmingham, Ala.: Religious Education Press, 1988.

Chapter Seven

How Goals Lead
to Volunteer Programs

To accomplish the goals and objectives of religious education a program is required. As noted in the last chapter, objectives must precede program planning, not be an afterthought. Goals also direct the program plan, a factor often overlooked by religious education directors. This is perhaps because most churches and other religious organizations already have a program and expect the director to set goals and objectives within the parameters of the existing program. This is unfortunate because the program is a means to an end, a way of accomplishing goals, which should be readily modified and even dispensed with if not relevant to the mission of the group and the consequent goals and objectives.

One important goal of a religious education program that uses volunteers is preservice sessions, to be considered in chapter twelve. This goal itself requires a program to be implemented. But the program serves as a means to the end of adequately prepared volunteers, and thus if the program is not meeting that goal it is not useful, at least in its present form.

Program development involves job design. Job descriptions should be planned ahead for religious education endeavors to ensure that each volunteer will know precisely what tasks are expected of him or her. This is not to imply that job descriptions must necessarily be rigid; overly rigid approaches can squelch creativity and maximal use of potential, producing frustration with higher dropout rates, not to mention more mediocre results.

Volunteer Roles and Job Descriptions

Job descriptions are the more fixed, assigned aspects of a task (although descriptions should be changed as needed), while roles are more emergent, generalized, and flexible aspects of one's position in an organization. What makes for a good job description?

Paul Ilsley and John Niemi emphasize six purposes of volunteer job descriptions:

1. Stating responsibilities of the job
2. Providing staff and supervisors with information about the job
3. Helping volunteers make informed decisions
4. Aiding in placement and recruitment of volunteers
5. Specifying training that may be needed to perform the job
6. Providing a basis for evaluation and supervision

Ilsley and Niemi emphasize that job descriptions should be developed subsequent to setting goals and prior to recruitment. Job descriptions should include:

1. Qualifications, including education and experience
2. Days and hours the volunteer is needed, and the degree of flexibility in these respects
3. How long a commitment is needed
4. Opportunities for training and learning new skills
5. Benefits, such as use of facilities on one's own time or snacks
6. Supportive services, such as child care, transportation, and insurance
7. Amount of responsibility involved

Several key questions regarding roles of participants should be considered in developing volunteer programs. These various roles must be defined overtly, preferably in writing, so that all involved will know what to expect of others and what others expect of them. Important questions regarding volunteer roles include:

1. What is the teacher's role? Does it include only verbal teaching, or does it also include the provision of materials, planning each detail of the lesson, and housekeeping tasks such as providing refreshments?
2. What is the distinctive role of an assistant among these possible role components?
3. Is the Sunday school superintendent or religious education director involved in a direct manner in regular activities? Are they supervisors, evaluators, or only resources?
4. Does the teacher, the religious education director, or the pastor decide on curriculum? Who orders the curriculum and when? Who decides what audiovisuals are needed and does the actual ordering?

How Organizations Deal with Tasks and Information

Needs and goals are fundamental to the development of volunteer organizations, including those that involve religious education. Yet it may also be helpful to step back and look at how organizations in general function. Karl Weick has developed a detailed theory as to how *any* organization functions, a theory with considerable relevance to religious education volunteer programs.

Weick maintains that processing information about a given task is a central function of organizations. The information about the task to be accomplished is complex and ambiguous, to a greater or lesser extent. In turn, the organization needs to respond with an equal degree of complexity and ambiguity.

The emphasis Weick places upon the complexity and ambiguity of tasks is clearly seen in religious education. What specifically do we mean by religious education? There are overwhelming possibilities in that phrase, everything from learning to recite sections of the Bible, to reflecting upon personal values, to comparing what different religions believe. James Michael Lee suggests a wide variety of contents are possible, such as cognitive, affective, nonverbal, and several others (see chapter thirteen). Even if we limit religious education to the cognitive content of theology, there is always the question of what theological topics are to be taught, in what order, to what ages, at what level of depth, with how many examples, from what theological perspective, using what educational procedures, and so on.

Weick emphasizes that the effective organization responds at the same level of complexity as the task. This probably does not consciously occur in many religious organizations. Decision makers rarely consider even a sampling of the many possibilities, but instead prefer to follow a preset curriculum that is often little more than a variation of what has gone before. This may be the easiest approach, but Weick would probably suggest that the result will necessarily be less than optimal.

Weick states that organizations use *cycles* of communication—behavior to accomplish a complex or ambiguous task. This involves an action by the person, a response to that action by a second person, and an adjustment by the first person. The more complex the task of the organization, the more important is the cycle of action, response, and adjustment because each cycle reduces the degree of complexity and ambiguity of the task. On the other hand, if the task is very familiar, an organization is more likely to use communication *rules* in which it searches for the standard, preformed answers it has discovered and used previously. Thus it becomes obvious that the initial analysis of the task is crucial to determine if using rules or cycles is the most appropriate response.

The cycles of communication-behavior indicate how volunteer religious organizations could develop their programs. Each cycle involves the assignment of meaning to the information received. The development of the religious education program needs to processed by individuals taking the action of interpreting the goal. These interpretations are evaluated by others in the organization, feedback is given, and adjustments made. As the cycles continue, it is likely that the ambiguity of the initial goal will be reduced (perhaps even for those who formed the goal).

One church used cycles to deal with the need in their community for ministry to children from single parent households. The very traditional congregation had no past experiences to draw from for developing such a ministry. As a result they initiated new approaches (cycles) to meet the needs.

Cycles may also occur in the use of information from research. Again, research is by its nature a complex process and results may be expressed in various ways. Furthermore, many different implications of findings are also possible. Thus the complexity of research related to education (and research related to volunteerism) needs to be cycled with a number of different individuals. Preferably these people should be qualified and educated to interpret at a level equal to the research, not oversimplifying or quickly limiting the analysis to a verifying of one's personal opinions and views. There should be several cycles, involving a number of people, for both the interpretation and application phases of analyzing relevant research.

The volunteer program itself also needs to be cycled. Efforts by volunteer coordinators, and volunteers themselves, constitute organizational actions, which require feedback and correction. Evaluating volunteers personally will be considered in chapter fourteen, while program evaluation is the subject of chapter twenty-four of this book.

Do rules for communication behavior have a place in religious education volunteerism? Weick seems to suggest a valid place for rules but only when a given task is very similar to a previous task. After the organization's efforts have been cycled several times, and the results maximized as a result, it is not always necessary to "reinvent the wheel" for every new volunteer or task.

For Weick, the organization may be understood as a method of adaptation which includes trying out various activities (teaching methods, for example), selecting those that work well and retaining beneficial actions for future use. This is as true for a religious organization as any other kind of organization. During the *enactment* stage the organization (religious or not) acquires information from the surrounding environment, assigning meaning to information received. Rules, cycles, or a combination of both are used to assign that meaning. The second stage, *selection*, involves making decisions about how well those rules and cycles have worked, perhaps repeating cycles if need be. The third stage, *retention*, involves gathering and storing information about how the organization responded (so it may be used in future, similar situations).

To illustrate these stages, *enactment* is represented by several different approaches to youth ministry. The director of the program might realize that there are many possible methods in the religious education of young people, such as providing entertainment and recreation, involvement in social action, and providing Bible studies. These approaches might have been acquired by reading books on youth work. The youth director might have interpreted the books by his prior experiences with young people. The selection stage would involve the recognition that, for him, the Bible study approach seems to work best, because he feels the recreational approach is not really religious and the social action approach will bring criticism from parents and church leaders. These conclusions may have come from his past attempts at using the other approaches (cycles) or from the recommendations of the church. The Bible study approach has been perceived as more successful to the youth director. The *retention* stage is when the youth director affirms that approach, making a mental note to never try the others again.

A number of other practical implications of this theory have been suggested by Krepps and Weick:

1. It is important for members of organizations to have plenty of communication with one another when dealing with complex tasks (see chapter twenty-two). Personal communication between religious education professionals, between volunteers, and between professional and volunteer staff is crucial to the effectiveness of the organization.

2. Organizations must be able to measure accurately the degree of complexity of a task so that appropriate communication-behavior cycles (or rules) can be put into action. For example, adding a new learner to the primary department requires a rule since educating primaries successfully is currently taking place. In contrast, developing a ministry to latchkey children may require cycles if the organization has never successfully accomplished this previously.

3. Managers should be more concerned about how members of an

organization relate and communicate with one another, rather than merely being concerned with the performance of individual people. Weick notes that relationships in organizations tend to be fluid and shift regularly. Religious educators should reject any notion that relationships and roles will be static and unchanging but rather look for important relational changes and make adjustments in light of those changes.

4. Teamwork must be stressed and regular meetings should be conducted that will encourage cooperation between members of an organization. The performance of the individual, while important, is only one aspect of the interactive process between administrators, other professionals, volunteers, and students. Functioning as a team is to be emphasized repeatedly in meetings, an important part of program climate (chapter twenty).

5. "Lessons from experience" should not be taken as absolutes, because they are actually interpretations of what occurred. They often tell more about the person's *reaction* to the experience than the experience itself. Perspective dominates, not objective recounting of what happened. Thus organizations will be more adaptable if they realize these are only plausible accounts that link past decisions with present situations. We must not reverence even the best religious education done in the past to the extent that we fail to see the distinctives in the new situation. We must also beware of the possibility, too, that the account of past efforts was faulty.

6. Finally Weick emphasizes that planning has far more importance for present decision making than it does in predicting what will happen in the future. Plans that change current behavior are obviously important in influencing the direction of the organization, but the results of those decisions are not always what is anticipated. Even the best plans are only tentative; they inform and direct current religious education decisions, but they may take the volunteer program in directions other than what is intended.

Program Delivery

Ilsley and Niemi note that there are at least three general ways in which the volunteer training program can be set up. These are individual, group, and community-based approaches. Many of their suggestions regarding the format of the volunteer program apply to religious education contexts in general, and thus can be viewed as alternative ways of delivering a religious education program.

Individual approaches include serving as an apprentice, becoming an intern, correspondence, using programed learning, and directed study.

In religious education, apprenticeship utilizes learning through the modeling of another individual. In scriptures we often observe Paul encouraging others to be like him. This is what James Michael Lee calls "lifestyle content," where the lifestyle is the material to be learned. Some Roman Catholics use retreats for this purpose, where the individual has few distractions and reflection upon life and meditation can be more easily accomplished. John Michael Talbot's Franciscan retreat in northern Arkansas is an example (many Protestants also make use of his retreat as well!). Another example of apprenticeship would be the one-to-one religious education of the DUI convict in chapter three.

An internship might include spending a summer in an inner-city context learning about the needs and potential of educating the needy. Internship overseas is another possibility.

Correspondence study is central to Theological Education by Extension (TEE) used by many denominations to educate pastors in localities that cannot afford to send pastors to college or seminary for training. Personal, one-to-one correspondence can also be the basis for religious education.

Programed instruction is an approach that can be combined with any of the above, as well as with group contexts, as a method of learning. Likewise, more independent individual study can be directed by a knowledgeable teacher when other approaches are inconvenient or inappropriate.

Group approaches include workshops, classes, conferences, or groups that meet for discussion. While these are the more traditional approaches to delivering religious education, they are important, viable alternatives yet today and for the foreseeable future.

Community approaches take place within the community as a whole. Religious education in this context would probably include church services and broader community religious education through the media, videotapes, and cassettes. Radio and television stations often allow for spot ads of a religious education nature as public service announcements.

Context

Program delivery not only relates to the approach to religious education, but also to the context. Ilsley and Niemi suggest that the following are needed for a good volunteer educational program:
1. Rooms in which to meet
2. Good lighting, heating, and cooling
3. Furniture that is appropriate
4. Any audiovisual equipment needed

5. Storage areas

6. Parking and transportation

7. Food

8. Library

9. Lack of extraneous noise

Programs require materials and facilities. This may already be provided in the church or parachurch budget and building, yet a specific form of religious education may require special provision in this area. For example, a home-based group (such as a Bible study or personal support group) may benefit from coffee and donuts. It is unrealistic for either the leader or the person owning the home to provide these continually. One cannot expect volunteers to effectively perform duties without adequate (safe, pleasant) surroundings, and adequate materials to perform the task. Overhead projectors, transparency-makers, videotape recorders and tapes, and visuals for hanging on walls and handing out in class should be planned ahead and may be an integral part of programs led by volunteers. Thus a supportive system involving a budget and perhaps personnel, becomes an important contingency for making volunteer religious education flourish. These may help motivate participants and group leaders as well, in or outside the church context.

Stages of Volunteer Program Development

Anne Smith developed a six-stage theory of volunteer program organizations. The following outline is taken from the brochure she wrote for the Center for Volunteer Development at Virginia Tech.

Stage 1 — Unmet needs. At this stage the volunteer organizations emerges from an existing group. People join because they match their needs and desires with the organization. Membership tends to be open to nearly anyone, communication is quite free, personal relationships predominate, and decisions are made through consensus. Patterns of leadership tend to be informal and emergent. Jobs and duties may be rotated between participants and leaders.

Stage 2 — An OK organization. Recruitment becomes important at this stage because of the desire to grow and change. More and more structure develops as the membership expands and roles are defined. Relationships are more secondary (they were more personal in stage one), and often subgroups tend to develop. Procedures and rules are established as tasks are more precisely defined.

At this stage volunteers may drop out because they become disillusioned with what is taking place and changing expectations. Unmet needs and failure to accomplish goals may also contribute to some leaving. The organization may require less of the person, and commitment by volunteers decreases.

Stage 3 — The honeymoon phase. By this point in the development of the volunteer organization the administrator is a paid employee who is responsible to the organization's board or staff. Bureaucracy develops, including committees that deal with changes and planning. Volunteers know specifically who is over them. With the initiation of paid staff conflicts may surface between volunteers and professionals. Yet volunteers are often trusting of the leadership and identify strongly with the organization. They develop friendships and attend meetings, sensing that the general organization is worthwhile. A few drop out because they are undermotivated or because they are not involved as actively as they would like.

Stage 4 — Disillusionment. At this point the organization has become more formal and centralized, resulting in volunteers that are less motivated and more disillusioned that before. Drop outs are more plentiful because the rewards for volunteers decreases and social/emotional support is absent. There is more domination by those in charge and an exclusiveness by the leaders and professionals which results in over-control of volunteers. Orientation tends to be lacking or absent and volunteer input and collaboration is unlikely. Leaders may hire special consultants, and planning comes to predominate.

Stage 5 — Rigidity. Stage five is a more extreme example of stage four. Often those in leadership can be influenced by specific groups within and outside the organization, but in general the structure hardens and goals fail to be accomplished. Volunteers drop out because they see themselves as having little or no influence upon procedures and policies as staff are doing more and more of the tasks. The largeness and complexity of the organization results in less communication and interaction, as well as increased alienation for volunteers.

Stage five is a crucial turning point. Smith points out that the organization may simply allow volunteers to leave, or it may even dissolve the volunteer program. Another alternative is to change the goals of the organization.

Stage 6 — Renewal. It is possible for the organization to rally from the crisis of stage five through self-examination. This often requires a renegotiation with volunteers which occurs on an ongoing basis. The organization must deal with dissatisfactions of volunteers and make adjustments to their policies and practices as required. Continual evaluation and review of the program is needed, as well as evaluation of volunteers so that further organizational crises can be avoided.

Conclusion

Goals become programs when there are adequate job descriptions and roles, tasks and information are interpreted and acted upon accurately, and when the approach and context are appropriate. These are all crucial to the activation and continuation of a first-rate religious education volunteers program.

For Further Reading

Ilsley, Paul, and John Niemi. *Recruiting and Training Volunteers*. New York: McGraw-Hill, 1981.

Kreps, G. L. "A Field Experimental Test and Revaluation of Weick's Model of Organizing." In *Communications Yearbook* 4, ed. D. Nimmo, pp. 389-398. New Brunswick, N.J.: Transaction Books, 1980.

Lee, James Michael. *The Content of Religious Instruction*. Birmingham, Ala.: Religious Education Press, 1985.

Smith, Anne. "The Developmental Process of Voluntary Associations." Blacksburg, Va.: Virginia Tech, Center for Volunteer Development, 1979.

Weick, Karl. *The Social Psychology of Organizing*, 2nd ed. New York: Random House, 1979.

Part III

Recruiting Religious
Education Volunteers

Chapter Eight

Where to Find Volunteers

Locating and recruiting good volunteers is an obvious priority for religious education programs. It should be noted that this step, while it is a priority for most churches, necessarily must follow the setting of goals, objectives, and program development. Without these preliminary phases (detailed in chapters six and seven) the religious organization may only be looking for warm bodies rather than appropriate people for the needed positions. "Warm bodies" probably will not stay in a volunteer position unless the components of that position fit reasonably well with their personal goals and interests (see chapter nine, as well as the religious educator lattice in chapter four).

A key task is to determine if a particular volunteer's interests and abilities are compatible with available religious education volunteer positions. Various criteria for positions need to be stated: relevant past experience required, previous education or training needed, and so on. In addition it may be helpful to state the likely outcomes of participating for the volunteer. These may include obtaining experience in a given area, acquiring skills in teaching or lesson preparation, acquiring a first-hand knowledge of child and adult development, preservice and inservice training, and so on. Outcomes for the volunteer may later serve as motivators for recruiting volunteers. The criteria stated for various positions available are integral to the recruitment process. From this point, matching volunteer competencies and potential with available openings is fundamental to effective recruitment.

Where is a person most likely to find volunteers? The obvious answer for religious education is in the church. While there is the potential for interchurch cooperative efforts for religious education activities such as sex education and other areas that require specific forms of expertise, generally the local church will be context for recruitment.

The Elderly

But who in the church can help? One important source is the older, retired person who may have more free time available than others. George Barna's research indicates that people over age fifty-five are far more likely to volunteer than other age groups in the church (he also finds that blacks, evangelicals, and married individuals volunteer the most in church). An entire book has been written on this topic, titled *Older Volunteers in Church and Community* by Paul Maves. Many of the elderly need to feel needed, have a lifetime of experience and knowledge to share through religious education efforts, and can still learn new skills (this is documented in research by Frances Courson and William Heward). Research by John Carney, Judith Dobson, and Russell Dobson indicates that senior citizen volunteers reading to and working with children as teacher assistants in public schools resulted in high self-concepts in children, as well as positive attitudes toward the volunteers and fewer disciplinary actions.

Year by year the number of people over age sixty-five continues to grow, a trend that will escalate as we move into the next century. Indeed, in comparison with other age ranges, the proportion of elderly considerably outdistances the others in rate of growth. We have a multitude of people who want and need to be used in volunteer efforts.

Maves reminds us of some of the ways the elderly are different from other volunteers. First, they have more time available to volunteer. Without a full-time job, they may come to feel useless and unneeded, and thus they are very receptive to an opportunity where they are needed. Second, they are most likely to volunteer for areas in which they already possess skills. Thus prime candidates for religious education efforts are former school teachers and other who have been involved in public and private education. These individuals are already equipped to teach, the religious education context only provides a new content to convey. Likewise, as seen in the RVICS example in chapter three, the retired may have important skills that can supply important supportive elements to religious education, even if they cannot perform the educational tasks themselves.

Third, the elderly have a great deal of training and experience they can draw upon. They can be good problem-solvers and may be more likely to resist impulsive decision making. For example, they may make good administrators of certain programs, even if they do not personally get involved in teaching aspects of religious education. They may make good evaluators of neophyte religious educators. They may be good participants on screening committees for other volunteers. Religious education committees should be peppered with gray-haired people. The elderly can make contributions at several levels of the religious educator lattice (see chapter four).

Fourth, Maves notes that the elderly may require flexible schedules. Older people may want the freedom to travel, or may require more time to rest between assignments. Fifth, while many retired people enjoy excellent health, special allowance may be needed for physical limitations. Some elderly may not want to drive cars at night, and they should not be expected to do strenuous activities. They may unexpectedly need hospital care, or simply wake up not feeling well enough to participate in the expected volunteer assignment.

Maves also lists some myths about elderly volunteers. First, age is not the same as aging. In fact, age is not even the best indicator of aging. In other words, people age at different rates, and thus some eighty-year-olds can do more than some sixty-year-olds. A second myth is that the elderly are less productive. In fact they can be depended upon more than some younger people. Third is the myth that they do not want active involvement in life. While some elderly believe this myth and thus disengage from everyday life, most older people are anxious to spend their lives in productive ways.

A fourth myth is that the elderly are rigid and unable to change, while in fact flexibility and being "set in their ways" is more a personality factor than it is an inevitable aspect of age. While some elderly individuals do develop rigid personalities because of physical changes in the brain, it is inaccurate to expect this simply because a person is older. A fifth myth is that the elderly generally become senile and revert to childish ways of thinking. This is an example of "ageism," prejudice against the elderly, which simply does not reflect the reality of most elderly people (Maves estimates senility affects 5 to 10 percent of the elderly). The final myth addressed by Maves is that the elderly are more carefree and serene. In fact they may endure more stress than others, because of loss of status (from retirement), loss of spouse and/or lifelong friends, and higher rates of poverty than is found in the general population.

In sum, the elderly are an important source of volunteers for religious education in the church or parachurch. In the writers' experience, even those in nursing homes may become valuable prayer volunteers, lead and contribute to Bible studies, possibly do some clerical work, and be active in other religious education efforts. While they may have special needs that should be addressed, as well as myths that they and volunteer coordinators alike will have to dispel, the elderly are a potentially invaluable segment of the population to use.

Young People

At the other end of the age spectrum are teenagers and preteens who may be helpful in volunteer efforts. They can provide a very helpful service in assisting with nursery work — there are still plenty of girls and young women in this age range that enjoy working with babies. Teenagers would fulfill the "subprofessional" role while adults in the nursery would more likely take the "paraprofessional" role (see the religious educator lattice in chapter four). However, they may need training and supervision if they are new to the task. Indeed, they may welcome such preparation because they will be able to do babysitting outside the church as a result. Such training may also be preparatory to certain paid positions in the church, such as child care during special services, in addition to their volunteer efforts in the nursery.

Toddlers need similar care. While formal religious education is inappropriate for very young children, proper care of youngsters is preparatory for later concepts of God and positive attitudes toward the church (see Donald Ratcliff's "Baby Faith: Infants, Toddlers and Religion").

Teenagers and some mature preteens may also be productive participants in planning and other religious education committee activities. Too often the leadership of the church feels they know what teens want and need, but a representative giving actual opinions of teens from the perspective of being a teenager may help the church avoid pointless expenditures and wasted time. Several teens should be represented on committees directly related to youth programs, but we should not overlook the potential for beneficial input to other broader committees as well.

In recent years there has been a trend in some areas toward peer teaching in the public schools. Peer teaching involves students teaching other students. Sometimes older students will teach those a grade or two younger, while in other circumstances peer teachers may be the same age as learners. Peers may effectively teach one another, one-to-one, in a personalized manner that may be even better than teaching by a formal instructor. Generally, however, peer teaching is an adjunct to standard instruction, introducing another perspective and approach to the content area. Religious education needs to explore the use of peer teaching by teen volunteers.

Some mature teenagers may be helpful as assistants to teachers at the preschool and elementary levels. As has been emphasized by Ronald Koteskey in his chapter of *Handbook of Youth Ministry*, teenagers are biologically adults. Society has taught them to be irresponsible, instead of taking on adult roles. In most non-Western cultures and throughout most of history (until a hundred years ago) they would have been considered fully adult. Encouraging them to volunteer for religious education activities is one way the church can work against the trend toward society encouraging irresponsible behavior in young people.

A study of nearly 50,000 ninth to twelfth graders reported by Peter Benson of the Search Institute indicates that young volunteers demonstrate more high self-esteem, develop more social skills, and increase in leadership and decision making abilities. Sixty-four percent of youth learned about volunteer opportunities at church, resulting in a greater likelihood for involvement in church and other structured activities than nonvolunteers. Young volunteers more likely affirm values of helping and compassion and are more likely to receive personal help from teachers, peers, and others. They were also more likely to have significant relationships with individuals outside their peer group, especially relationships with non-peers involved in service to others. More girls than boys volunteer at every grade level, but both gradually decline in involvement as they move through their high school years.

It might also be noted that college students are good recruits for volunteer efforts. Not only may they have the time flexibility to take on volunteerism, but they may even be able to gain academic credit or obtain experience relevant to their eventual profession (e.g., teaching, administration).

Other Likely Candidates

Volunteerism is, of course, also appropriate for individuals in other age ranges. Children may volunteer to help cut out decorations for Sunday school classrooms, or perhaps want to help with some housekeeping tasks. They may be able to volunteer after school to help prepare for weekend or evening religious education activities. Through the latter, "latch-key" children may help the religious education program and at the same time get needed adult supervision. Alternately, children may volunteer with their parents for activities such as making telephone calls to encourage people to attend religious education activities.

Religious education may involve teaching new parents how to care for their expected or already born child. In the past such training may have been provided by the grandparents or other members of the extended family, but increasingly new parents are left on their own to learn and perform these tasks. Books may help, but personal instruction and discussion are often needed. Older parents may volunteer to help with this instruction, perhaps bringing babies to the training to model how to provide care. This care is crucial not only to emotional well-being, but also spiritual formation (again, see the Ratcliff article). These volunteers may be able to teach a parenting class, not only for new parents but for any age. They may work as a team, with a new leader each week (perhaps participating as group members the other weeks). Or they may serve as assistants to an main instructor who leads the class. Another possibility is that experienced parents may train teenagers to take care of infants and toddlers during church activities.

Finding volunteers to do religious education tasks on weekends and evenings is not as difficult as finding people during normal working hours on weekdays. Where can volunteers be found for these positions? Steve McCurley and Sue Vineyard offer some suggestions:

1. Find people who are unemployed. This could include not only those who cannot find a job, but also those with disabilities, the retired, full-time housewives, and those who are independently wealthy.

2. Those who are self-employed or who are employers may have more flexible schedules allowing for volunteering during these hours.

3. Those who do not work year-round may be available, such as outside employees in cold climates, teachers, etc.

4. Some work during nontraditional working hours, such as those on the night shift, students, or those who work weekends.

5. Some employees have unusual schedules because they work irregular hours, such as substitute teachers or those on-call for their jobs.

6. There are also those who can possibly do volunteer work while they perform their regular job. For example, during slack periods a secretary might make calls inviting others to church activities or could type materials for a class.

Those with low incomes may also be likely recruits. McCurley and Vineyard have suggestions for reaching these individuals:

1. Use visual rather than verbal materials.

2. Organize their volunteer work around "job development" possibilities. Examples of volunteers who have successfully become employed may help.

3. Self-help should be emphasized.

4. Reimburse or minimize expenses.

5. Attempt to match the backgrounds of recruiters/interviewers with volunteers.

6. Keep paperwork and jargon to a minimum.

7. Emphasize personal contact in recruitment.

8. Keep delays in processing to a minimum.

This section certainly does not exhaust the possibilities of the age ranges and contexts for obtaining volunteers. Volunteers can be virtually any age and in any location. Yet it must be acknowledged that in most cases religious education volunteers must come from within the church, to minimize undesirable factors. Even then, screening is needed (see chapter ten). Volunteers should be sought from both traditional sources (those in early and middle adulthood) and nontraditional sources (the elderly, the young, the unemployed, and those on low incomes).

Who Should Do the Recruiting?

The apparent answer to this question is that volunteer coordinators, religious education directors, members of religious education boards, pastors and priests, and other professionals are good recruiters. While they may be good recruiters, indeed even indispensable recruiters, we must not overlook the fact that the best advertising for volunteers is the satisfied volunteer. Word of mouth recruitment by those who have had happy volunteer experiences is the ideal, though this will probably need to be supplemented with recruitment by professionals as well. The importance of word of mouth efforts by satisfied volunteers underscores the importance of climate and high motivation in the volunteer program, thus these are crucial elements that have been underscored throughout this book. Those who coordinate volunteer religious education programs need to encourage ongoing volunteers to help locate willing people who can help in needed areas. This will not only provide a source of volunteers, but help current volunteers become more involved in the overall religious education effort.

For Further Reading

Barna, George. *What Americans Believe*. Ventura, Calif.: Regal, 1991.

Benson, Peter, and Eugene Roehlkepartain. "Kids Who Care." *Source* 7:3, (1992), pp. 1-3.

Carney, John, Judith Dobson, and Russell Dobson. "Using Senior Citizen

Volunteers in the Schools." *Journal of Humanistic Education and Development* 25 (March 1987), pp. 136-143.

Courson, Francis and William Heward. "Using Senior Citizens in the Special Education Classroom." *Academic-Therapy* 24 (May 1989), pp. 525-532.

Koteskey, Ronald. "The Social Invention of Adolescence." In *Handbook of Youth Ministry*, ed. Donald Ratcliff, pp. 42-69. Birmingham, Ala.: Religious Education Press, 1991.

Maves, Paul. *Older Volunteers in Church and Community.* Valley Forge, Pa.: Judson, 1981.

McCurley, Steve, and Sue Vineyard. *101 Tips for Volunteer Recruitment.* Downers Grove, Ill.: Heritage Arts, 1988.

Ratcliff, Donald. "Baby Faith." *Religious Education* 87 (Winter 1992), pp. 117-126.

Chapter Nine

Encouraging Them to Volunteer

The Old Testament book of Jonah reveals the fascinating account of recruiting an unwilling volunteer. It seems that God selected Jonah as the volunteer spokesman to the city of Ninevah, but Jonah chose instead to board a ship for Tarshish. Relying on innovative recruitment techniques, God orders up a big fish to temporarily consume Jonah and thus convince him of the importance of volunteering.

While most religious education recruiters lack the power to employ such recruitment devices as strategically placed fish, many would welcome the results God prompted in Jonah. Mark Senter speaks for countless church leaders when in the introduction of his book, *Recruiting Volunteers in the Church*, he suggests that recruitment constituted his greatest area of need for preparation in ministry. Anyone who has faced the recruitment task has known the apprehension of asking, and the rejection of hearing, "No!"

Three topics addressed in this chapter may help in the recruitment of religious education volunteers. These include:

1. Motivating people to volunteer
2. Developing the environment for volunteering
3. Recruitment strategies

Using Motivation to Recruit

Conventional wisdom has long asserted that people volunteer primarily for altruistic reasons. An offshoot of that basic thought is debt repayment as the primary motivating factor. Were such theories altogether accurate, recruitment would become a simple matter of packaging the need so effectively or increasing the sense of debt to such heightened levels that recruitment becomes a simple task of signing up willing volunteers.

In fact, some religious organizations do operate their recruiting programs on just such a premise. One church convinced a layman to volunteer to develop a bus ministry in the low income government housing project of his city. The volunteer had no particular skill or interest in such a ministry. His upper-middle-class background proved less than effective preparation for the task. Further, the church offered no training for the ministry. When asked candidly about his involvement, this volunteer explained, "Pastor just helped me to see that the needs were so great—surely somebody must help these children." While the need may have warranted attention, one wonders about the nature of the recruiting practice.

Another volunteer, forced to deal with her real motivations for teaching when attendance at her Sunday school class steadily declined, declared, "I'm just so grateful for what Jesus did for me, that I have to repay Him. This is the best way I know." While her appreciation is admirable, her sense of debt failed to provide adequate teaching resources. A better technique would have more effectively served the coordinator of volunteers who recruited her.

In the pragmatic society of the 1990s, perhaps a more realistic theory for what motivates people to volunteer has emerged. One possibility, social exchange theory, first appeared in the late 1950s as a result of the work of J.W. Thibaut and H.H. Kelly. They assert that individual behavior can best be understood in terms of rewards and costs. Individuals evaluate any particular behavior in terms of the anticipated benefits of involvement offset by the anticipated liabilities. For example, a prospective adult Sunday school teacher might think through whether or not to volunteer like this:

Advantages of teaching	Disadvantages of teaching
1. Feeling of being useful	1. Six hours per week preparation time
2. Forces personal in-depth study	2. Fear of speaking in public
3. Get better acquainted with class members	3. Hard to resign later

According to the theory, the prospect will weigh these relative advantages and disadvantages, arriving at a "comparison level." If, for example, the fear of public speaking is intense in this particular person, the resulting low comparison level will cause the rejection of the volunteer position.

In addition, the prospect may consider other avenues of service which would provide similar benefits at less cost. These form a "comparison level of alternatives" which also is considered. Clearly, several alternatives could emerge for consideration at the same time. Presumably, the potential volunteer will select that course of action which offers the highest comparison level. The effective recruiter will increase the perception of rewards and decrease the perception of costs for any given task and any particular volunteer. This will involve establishing the proper recruiting climate and, on occasion, dealing with objections.

Eileen Starr studied the volunteer motivations of Sunday school teachers in Anchorage Alaska evangelical churches. While the location of the study must necessarily restrict quick generalizations, the findings are suggestive for other religious education contexts as well. Starr found that the primary motivations for most of the teachers were (in order) affiliation, achievement, and spiritual altruism, while duty/guilt, intrinsic motivation, and leadership/power motivations were secondary and often completely absent. Women volunteers were more likely to cite affiliation as their most important motivation, while men were more likely to cite achievement as the central motivation. Age of the teacher, age of the persons taught, teaching experience, degree of pastoral involvement and encouragement, and the theology of the church (Wesleyan vs. Pentecostal vs. Reformed) made no significant difference in motivation.

Starr found these Sunday school teachers, as a group, to be highly motivated toward involvement with others (affiliation) and wanting to improve and desirous of accomplishing something important (achievement). While these differed by gender, most of the teachers cited spiritual growth and learning as important motivators as well.

Developing the Environment for Volunteering

John Naisbitt, in his famous book *Megatrends*, underscores the long-term change that has occurred in society toward "high touch." "High touch" is contrasted with, and an increasingly important adjunct to "high tech" (high technology) that dominates modern society. Naisbitt means that personal contact between persons is now more important than ever before. This is because of the increased loneliness and isolation people feel. We will consider this further in chapter twenty-six.

This trend would suggest two things for volunteerism. First, "high touch" should be integral to the volunteer effort. An emphasis upon personal contact in religious education would be helpful to recruitment efforts. Good religious education involves the personal element, and this should be highlighted. Second, the process of recruitment itself should be "high touch." While high tech approaches to recruitment can be valuable in some situations, personal contact with potential volunteers is far better than distanced approaches.

Consider the typical appeal for volunteers in many churches. The pastor or religious education director probably announces from the pulpit the great need for a volunteer to take care of the nursery or teach the boy's junior high catechism class. This appeal may involve a bit of manipulation by the use of guilt ("What have you done for the church/God this week?") or more direct coercion ("If no one volunteers, we may have to close down the nursery"). An alternative to the public announcement approach is to place one or more announcements in the church bulletin or on an announcement board somewhere in the church.

These approaches, however, are hardly "high touch" (nor are they even "high tech"). People are likely to volunteer only if already highly motivated, or they may volunteer for the wrong reasons (e.g., guilt). These reasons will probably not be enough to keep them involved. They also tend to demean the position — guilt and coercion may communicate the message the job is not worth doing. Furthermore, it manipulates the volunteer, since the unspoken message is, "It will not get done if you do not do it." Fred Wilson gives research evidence that guilt makes some people *less* likely to be involved (see chapter eleven). Finally, it also may result in people who you do not want volunteering, yet undesirables may be the only people who volunteer.

Instead of begging, more of a personal appeal may be more appropriate and effective. Sometimes word of mouth approaches can be useful, where key people in the church can personally communicate to friends and acquaintances the needs that are available. An alternative is to use inventories of abilities and spiritual gifts that may indicate who could potentially be skilled in specific religious education activities. George Barna emphasizes that we should seek out the person's interests and abilities, then steer them to existing or new positions in the church where they can exercise those abilities. "High touch" demands that we begin where the person is in terms of interests, needs, and expertise and then individually suggest to them possible areas in which they can minister effectively.

This does not mean that public presentations are to be dismissed. However, such presentations should not be an announcement of positions available, but rather be carefully planned events that will sensitize specific groups of people to needs as well as their talents and potential. A well-done video on youth ministry may help adults see how vital this area is to the future of the church. Describing a teacher-training seminar appropriate to the listeners' level on the religious education lattice, and without obligation to volunteer afterward, may serve as a means of personal growth for participants as well as a screening device by volunteer coordinators. Such a seminar would further sensitize people to needs generally (not just those specific to that church), and those who show promise can be approached individually by seminar leaders for specific positions. The fact that a person attends such a seminar would indicate interest, thus part of the seminar activities should involve evaluation of ability and potential.

Recruitment Approaches

Steve McCurly and Rick Lynch identify two basic types of recruiting processes. They label "warm body recruitment" as that process which searches for a general volunteer. In effect, any warm body could handle the task at hand. "Targeted recruitment," they suggest, becomes necessary when the task requires specific skills or abilities. Sweeping up after Vacation Bible School, or answering the office telephone provide examples of warm body positions. Targeted recruitment, on the other hand, becomes necessary when searching for a church treasurer, or someone with teaching skills.

McCurly and Lynch suggest six questions the recruiter of targeted individuals will want to ask. These include:

1. What is the job that needs to be done?
2. Who would want to do the job?
3. Where will they be found?
4. How should we communicate with them?
5. What are their motivational needs?
6. What will we say to them?

Every recruiter has a unique procedure for answering these questions and thus for stimulating volunteers to step forward. Hence, a host of methods exists.

Senter believes that recruiting encompasses a year-long process. He suggests activities for each month to assist in developing a recruitment program. This "recruitment calendar" becomes a guide for day-to-day recruiting activities.

An unpublished author, Howard Mayne, also declares year-round recruiting as the most effective. In addition, he suggests that the personal visit constitutes the only truly effective recruiting mechanism in his experience. Mayne further declares the importance of making the recruitment calls in teams of two after phoning ahead for an appointment.

The pastor of a mid-sized Midwestern congregation affirms the importance of personal appeal but employs that contact differently. Annually, in the fall of the year, he leads the congregation in a commitment service at the altar of the church. Each participant studies a comprehensive list of assignments which must be completed during the coming year. These tasks include such diverse elements as pulpit supply, Sunday school teacher, host or hostess for evangelists, prayer supporter for missionaries, and cook for the Sunday school teacher appreciation banquet. The key to successful recruiting in this case lies in the well-thought-out need for volunteers and the assumption that everyone in the congregation will volunteer for some task.

The latter assumption characterized a central Kentucky congregation that placed a heavy emphasis on the priesthood of all believers. This church identified itself as a place where "all members are ministers." The idea of a nonvolunteer was hardly an option.

Yet another congregation stretched the concept of total member involvement to the point of requiring volunteer work for membership. In addition to declaring their affirmation of theological views and allegiance to the church, prospective members publicly declare their intended ministry within the congregation as a membership vow. Far from limiting the number of persons willing to unite with the church, this congregation mushroomed in size under such stringent demands.

Each of these recruitment techniques begins at the point of organizational need. First, successful recruiters suggest that management must determine and communicate what tasks require volunteers. Some effective recruiters help potential volunteers discover their unique abilities or gifts, then tailor ministry to those discoveries.

Hugh Smith, a South Dakota Roman Catholic, has developed a "Spiritual Gifts Inventory" to help his parishioners discover how they might more fully and effectively participate in the life of the parish. The Inventory utilizes 125 questions designed to point the participant to one or more of the 25 strengths being tested. Smith reports a tremendous level of discovery and involvement among participants.

Similarly, United Methodist Kenneth Kinghorn uses a 200 question survey, described in his book *Discovering Your Spiritual Gifts*. His test considers twenty general gifts identified in scripture. Again, the approach seeks to engage laity in service by assisting in the discovery of ability.

Leaders who choose to utilize these inventories, or one of several others available, will want to carefully follow up by assisting participants in the creation of a volunteer ministry corresponding to their own ability.

Using the spiritual gifts approach, rather than warm body or targeting approaches discussed earlier, may well mean there will be gaps in a particular church's total ministry. The directed enthusiasm of volunteers will compensate, however, in many cases.

What If There Still Are No Volunteers?

Sometimes even the very best approaches still leave unfilled positions. Senter suggests asking four questions at that point. These are:

1. Drop?
2. Harm?
3. Alternatives?
4. Dramatize?

The one-word question "drop?" points to evaluating the need for the unstaffed ministry. If no one willingly steps forward, perhaps abilities are being better utilized elsewhere.

"Harm?" indicates asking what harm might come from operating the existing ministry, but without one volunteer. Could operations be streamlined to minimize the need for the position in question?

Focusing on "alternatives?" may point to places where duplicate programs can be eliminated or where a slightly different format would produce ample volunteer staff.

Finally, the question "dramatize?" implies dramatically letting the congregation know of the vacancy and the impact of failing to fill that vacancy. One church whose recruiting efforts failed to produce an adult leader for junior high youth developed a documentary-video of troubled young people in their community. The implicit question, "Who will prevent our church's teens from these disasters?" produced results.

While the recruiter of today's volunteers may not provide giant fish to convince prospects, some attention to why people volunteer, the environment of volunteering, and recruitment strategies can produce significant results. Other aspects of motivation will be considered in chapters eleven, fifteen, and seventeen, while the environment is the topic of chapter twenty.

For Further Reading

Barna, George. *User-Friendly Churches*. Glendale, Calif.: Regal, 1991.
Kinghorn, Kenneth C. *Discovering Your Spiritual Gifts*. Wilmore, Ky.: Francis Asbury Press, 1981.

Mayne, Howard. "Church Management Manual." McComb, Ohio: McComb United Methodist Church, 1986.

McCurly, Steve, and Rick Lynch. *Essential Volunteer Management*. Downers Grove, Ill.: V.M. Systems/Heritage Arts, 1989.

Naisbitt, John. *Megatrends*. New York: Warner, 1982.

Senter III, Mark. *Recruiting Volunteers in the Church*. Wheaton, Ill.: Victor, 1990.

Smith, Hugh. "You Are Gifted." *Pastoral Life* (June 1981), pp. 10-17.

Starr, Eileen. *A Description of the Motivations for Teaching Identified by Lay Volunteer Sunday School Teachers*. Ed.D. dissertation, Deerfield, Ill.: Trinity Evangelical Divinity School, 1989. Micropublished by Theological Research Exchange Network, Portland, Ore., 1989.

Thibaut, J.W., and H.H. Kelly. *The Social Psychology of Groups*. New York: Wiley, 1959.

Wilson, Fred. "Recruiting the Baby Boomer for Ministry." *Christian Education Journal* 11 (1990), pp. 51-68.

Chapter Ten

Screening Prospective Volunteers

Perhaps it goes without saying, but not every prospective volunteer is appropriate for the desired religious education job. An individual may lack key abilities, competencies, or potential to learn. The person indicating interest may have personality difficulties that rule him or her out for the position. They may lack spiritual qualities considered essential for the opening. How can leaders screen prospects in order to find the right person and turn away the wrong person?

First of all, recruitment must be done the right way. We have previously emphasized that public announcements of openings may attract people who want to be involved but for one reason or another should not participate. The volunteer coordinator faces a difficult situation when there obviously exists a great need and yet the potential volunteer is woefully inappropriate.

Sometimes seminars screen potential volunteers. At the very least seminars can help overcome misconceptions prospects may have. In addition, if seminars include performance objectives and role-playing, this provides a means of screening as well.

The Welcome Packet

Judy Wortley recommends that churches develop a packet of information for volunteers so they can become acquainted with the religious education volunteer program. She recommends that the packet include:

1. *A letter of welcome*

2. A sheet for *personal information* (or the application to be considered in detail shortly)

3. The *description* of the specific volunteer position being considered

4. A copy of the *doctrinal statement* of the church or religious organization

5. The *philosophy of ministry* (perhaps the mission statement might be included as well)

6. *Schedules* for preservice or inservice sessions, or a schedule of future staff meetings

7. A *contract* or "covenant" (see chapter eleven)

8. *Other important materials*, such as descriptions of how to do the religious education task being considered, handbooks, etc.

Wortley also suggests letting prospective volunteers observe the activity they have been asked to do. While she recommends this take place after the interview, there is perhaps even more reason for them to observe early in the screening process. More churches and religious organizations should consider including systematic observations of the religious education behavior desired so potential volunteers can see what they are being asked to do. One-way mirrors may help keep observers from interfering in the religious education process, but giving pointers on how to keep from distracting students receiving religious education can make observers relatively unobtrusive.

The Application

Some sort of formal application is desirable with volunteers. This need not be lengthy and detailed but is valuable because it allows the prospect to reflect carefully on relevant past experiences and upon the competencies relevant for the position. Some churches go further by contacting employers (present and past) and other references to determine if the candidate is appropriate. One large church even has FBI checks on their volunteers!

Paul Ilsley and John Niemi recommend that the application form include information in five general categories. These include background information, education, experience, interests, and goals/expectations.

Background information includes the prospective volunteer's full name, complete address, and telephone number. Many choose to obtain not only the home telephone, but the work telephone and the spouse's work telephone numbers as well. This section can also include the time and days available, as well as any means of transportation they have available.

Education should include degrees and major/minor areas, but also a listing of coursework relevant to the volunteer task. Volunteers should also have the opportunity of including nontraditional education, such as workshops and other specialized training.

VOLUNTEER APPLICATION

Name _____ Age _____ Gender _____

Address _____

Telephone (home) _____ (work) _____

    (spouse at work) _____

Education: high school diploma? _____ college: _____ years

    college degrees: _____ majors/minors: _____

    coursework related to volunteer position: _____
_____

    other education (workshops, specialized training): _____
_____

    plans for future education (if any): _____

Travel experience related to volunteer task: _____

Current employer/address: _____

Previous employer/address: _____

Other employment related to volunteer task: _____

What are your long-term and short-term career goals? _____
_____

Prior volunteer experience (include name and address of coordinator/s)
_____
_____

Personal references: _____
_____

Member of a church? _____ Name/address: _____

Church & address you attend most often: _____

Do you attend: ____ weekly or more ____ once or twice/month ____ less

Days and times available _____
_____

On a separate sheet of paper, write one or more paragraphs on each of the following topics:

    1. Describe your own past experiences of receiving religious education, beginning in childhood.

    2. Describe your interests and hobbies.

    3. Describe why you want to volunteer for this position.

    4. Describe what skills and knowledge you have related to religious education.

    5. List what you expect to accomplish and how you expect to accomplish it through this volunteer position.

Note that the questionaires may be reproduced without permission. In most cases, not all of the above questions will be needed in the questionaire, thus feel free to use only sections needed and/or adapt questions to your specific purpose.

Experience includes not only prior and current employment but also volunteer roles held in the past. Ask for the names and addresses of employers and volunteer coordinators, for follow up. Travel experiences may also be relevant to religious education tasks. References should be requested primarily to verify experience and personal information. Past experiences in their own religious education during childhood and adulthood can be very helpful here. Church membership and frequency of attendance are crucial issues to include.

A broad-ranging section on interests should include hobbies. Some areas of interest may seem irrelevant to the prospective volunteer, yet prove invaluable once he or she begins to serve. A separate section on volunteer interests should include an open-ended question about why they want to volunteer. Several questions should inquire into the skills and knowledge related to religious education.

Solicit career goals, both immediate and long-term, as well as plans for future education which may also indicate career goals. Finally, be sure to ask about their expectations from the volunteer organization.

Interviewing

Crucial to successful recruitment is an effective interview with the prospect. Paul Maves emphasizes the importance of an appointment made in advance for the interview, which can take place either in the prospect's home or at the religious organization. Mark Senter recommends the following guidelines for interviewing, which will be elaborated upon shortly:

1. Interview in person and privately
2. Provide the prospective volunteer with a list of questions that will be asked during the interview, so they can be reflected upon adequately
3. Follow a standard format. Senter recommends:
   A. personal religious experience
   B. prior training
   C. prior experience
   D. hobbies and other special interests
   E. the prospect's expectations

F. any fears they may have

G. ministry preferences

4. Do not place volunteer merely according to the area of greatest need

5. A period of observation should follow the interview

6. Obtain feedback from likely coworkers on the prospective volunteer

7. The interview should lead to either placement or being informed as to why they were not placed

It is important that interviewing be done face-to-face and not via telephone in that many aspects of the prospective volunteer can be observed in person that are inaccessible over the telephone. This includes their body language, physical characteristics that may have a bearing on the position, and other attitudes, motives, and beliefs which may emerge during the interview but can be overlooked in an application. The interview should include their relevant past experience (to help determine competencies), why they are interested in the present position, and perhaps an account of their prior religious experiences, membership, and church participation.

Steve McCurley and Sue Vineyard offer a number of other suggestions for interviewing:

First, indirect questions should be used. For example, "What religious education positions have you held in the past?" or "Where have you volunteered previously?" "What kind of work do you enjoy doing (or do not enjoy)?" may help the coordinator match interests with religious education positions available. Questions about the family, decision-making skills, time available, and desired supervision help in making screening decisions.

During the interview, attempt to avoid interruptions. Actively listen, answering questions as openly and honestly as possible. Avoid promises if you are not yet certain of placement. Friendliness is important, but do not overdo the amount of talking done; give them plenty of opportunity to share their feelings and reveal their questions and inner motivations.

If the prospect mentions difficulties with the potential assignment, discuss these in detail attempting to remove some objections. However, be sure that the opening is described honestly; hiding undesirable aspects of the job until they have made a commitment is asking for short-term, unmotivated participants. Do not assume interviewees understand the tasks involved; avoid assumptions in general.

McCurley and Vineyard also describe a number of pitfalls to avoid in interviewing potential recruits. Try to avoid:

1. Questions asked in a leading manner
2. Hasty decisions
3. Prematurely terminating the interview
4. Allowing the conversation to move off topic
5. Becoming prejudicial
6. Providing too little information
7. Basing the decision entirely on personality
8. Not really listening to answers
9. Dishonesty about requirements, responsibilities, etc.
10. Naivete; volunteers may not be telling the entire truth

Volunteers will usually want to ask a number of questions but may be unwilling to inquire overtly. Be sure to address these during the interview. They include *first* the specifics of the task, including authority and accountability. *Second*, potential volunteers also want to know the amount of time needed for the task — try to estimate the required number of hours per week and the flexibility of time requirements. *Third*, the specific needs and benefits to those receiving the religious education should be detailed to the potential volunteer. *Finally*, the organization's accountability should be addressed by discussing how money is spent, others who have worked with the organization, and a brief history of the group. If potential volunteers have the answers to these questions, they are more likely to be committed to the group and feel the interviewer is not trying to hide things from them.

Ilsley and Niemi consider prediction as one of the purposes of the interview. The attitudes and behavior gained from past experiences best predict future behavior and attitudes, although they are far from perfect. The interviewer should attempt to discover work habits, interest in learning, abilities at cooperation, and other important details in making an adequate prediction for future volunteer efforts. The amount of time spent at prior volunteer experiences and the reason for leaving prior employment may also help yield crucial information.

As noted in the next chapter, it is not always necessary to press for a decision during the interview. Maves suggests giving time to think over the decision and then checking back with them (perhaps several times) for their decision.

Committee Involvement

Oftentimes the screening process requires the use of a committee. While the interviewer provides helpful information to this group, the religious education committee may make the vital decision. This has many possible benefits. The responsibility for the decision rests not just on one person's shoulders, therefore the coordinator is less likely to be accused of personally disliking the potential volunteer. Others on the committee may have further information on the person being considered. While one person may accept the task of interviewing, others may contact friends, employers, and organizations for which the person may have previously volunteered.

Reginald McDonough recommends that five, six, or seven members elected by the church form the committee and be responsible for all volunteer appointments. He lists six responsibilities of the committee:

1. *Selecting, interviewing, and enlisting all program leaders*
2. *Screening all other volunteers* before leaders may enlist their efforts
3. *Deciding where leaders need to be placed,* using the priorities of the church and the talents of the leaders as guidelines
4. *Helping leaders find and recruit volunteer leaders,* as well as helping leaders recruit other volunteers
5. *Bringing eligible volunteers before the church body* for possible election to the proposed position (if consistent with church polity)
6. *Proposing certain individuals for membership on church committees*

McDonough recommends that this committee function all year long, preparing to fill vacancies for the next cycle of enlistments. Soliciting new directors of programs should begin five or more months prior to the beginning of their term, says McDonough, thus allowing plenty of time for orientation and training.

Follow-Up

A good follow-up to the interview, including the contacting of others who have worked closely with the potential volunteer previously, is crucial. One religious organization used a volunteer to help with public relations. Within a few months the volunteer was found to have a hidden agenda in that work; he became sexually involved with a married secretary and suddenly abandoned his job by moving to another state when his actions were discovered. Upon contacting his former employers, too late for it to do any good, it was discovered he had a long history of sexual indiscretions in religious organizations.

A second example concerns a church who felt desperate for a pastor, and thus the first serious applicant was accepted with little or no investigation of prior pastoral experiences. Within six months he was dismissed, following a series of explicit sermons on sexual perversions.

For Further Reading

Ilsley, Paul, and John Niemi. *Recruting and Training Volunteers*. New York: McGraw-Hill, 1981.

McCurley, Steve, and Sue Vineyard, *101 Tips for Volunteer Recruitment*. Downers Grove, Ill.: Heritage Arts, 1988.

Maves, Paul. B. *Older Volunteers in Church and Community*. Valley Forge, Pa.: Judson, 1981.

McDonough, Reginald. *Working with Volunteer Leaders in the Church*. Nashville: Broadman, 1976.

Senter III, Mark. *Recruiting Volunteers in the Church*, rev. ed. Wheaton, Ill.: Victor, 1990.

Wortley, Judy. *The Recruiting Remedy*. Elgin, Ill.: Cook, 1990.

Chapter Eleven

Getting Commitments from Volunteers

Commitment is essential to obtaining responsible volunteers. Ongoing commitment comes with involvement in the program, but during recruitment a definite commitment to the religious education task must be obtained. Dependable paraprofessionals and subprofessionals (see chapter four) are crucial for quality results.

At the end of the interview, assuming all has gone well and the person is qualified for the position, the interviewer should ask for a decision. Of course this assumes that references, employers, and relevant others have been contacted prior to the interview and have given positive evaluations of the prospect. If this has not been done before the interview, the request for commitment should be deferred until the prospective volunteer has been checked out. Even if the interview has been less than perfect, with the potential volunteer expressing considerable reservation, you should still ask for a commitment. Hesitancy by the prospect may not stem from unwillingness to participate, but rather represent an attempt to be honest in expressing doubts and questions. As noted previously, the actual response of the prospect need not be given immediately, but he or she needs to know a decision is expected.

The Agreement

Developing and signing a formal agreement is important to commitment, say Paul Ilsley and John Niemi. While they find this less important for religious volunteer efforts, it bears consideration even within this context. The agreement should ideally be a written document that includes conditions of the volunteer work, benefits (both material and personal), possible training, performance standards such as hours required, length of the commitment, indicators of adequate performance, and any training or meetings required. The agreement is closely related to the components of the job description.

The agreement sets the basis not only for what is expected of the volunteer by the organization, but also what is expected of the organization by the volunteer. While it falls short of a legal document (a disclaimer should be included to keep it from becoming such), the agreement helps to set the basis for evaluation and supervision and guides the volunteer towards meeting expectations. An example of a short-term contract is found in chapter sixteen.

Not only should specific job tasks and benefits be included, but also some statements related to the environment (or climate — see chapter twenty). For example, Ilsley and Niemi suggest including these expectations of the organization: *being treated respectfully*, a social climate marked by *openness, recognition* for positive accomplishment, *fair evaluations and supervision, and valuing the volunteer's opinion.*

Ilsley and Niemi also include these expectations of the volunteer: *a commitment to the standards and goals* of the organization, manifesting a attitude of *diligence and wanting to serve, dedication* to the tasks, *being discrete* in communicating with those outside the organization (confidentiality to the degree needed), and *loyalty.*

Other areas that might be included in the agreement are considered at length by Ilsley and Niemi. A religious organization may want to include a few of these ideas in the agreement (including very many may be seen as threatening to some volunteers!). From the organization the commitment might include:

1. *Cooperation*, including the providing of access to buildings and leaders, a safe environment, opportunities for interaction, leadership, or decision making, information accessibility, having a task that is significant and challenging, opportunities to learn, and becoming aware of constraints within the organization.

2. *Supportive benefits* such as being reimbursed for classes taken, travel expenses, or child care.

3. *Learning opportunities* through preservice and inservice education, formal education, special conferences or seminars, access to individualized instruction, and exposure to an environment conducive to learning.

From the volunteer the commitment agreement would include elements such as:

1. *Requirements of the organization* including attendance at training sessions and meetings, keeping good records, knowledge of how the orga-

nization operates, knowing one's obligations and privileges, coordinating activities according to the organization's guidelines and lines of authority, and knowing the goals of the program.

2. *Commitment of time* such as length of the commitment and amount of time each week required.

3. *Meeting standards* by knowing requirements, meeting goals, understanding the criteria by which one is evaluated, knowing what competencies are necessary for a task and where one has limitations.

Dealing with Objections

In spite of the best efforts on the part of the volunteer recruiter to set the proper tone conducive to volunteering, some prospects will express reservations. Some differences of opinion exist as to how, in general, to best deal with objections. One pastor wrote in an unpublished training manual, "If the response is negative, don't take 'no' for an answer." The writer goes on to describe techniques designed to convince the candidate to volunteer.

While circumstances exist where a bit more information may change a negative response to positive, it generally seems appropriate to accept the decision of the potential volunteer, even if that decision is "no." On the other hand, some objections really indicate a problem other than unwillingness to volunteer. These objections, when properly addressed, often become opportunities to enhance the overall volunteer program.

For example, the most common objection, "I'm really not qualified," provides an opportunity to discuss the training aspects of the volunteer program. Responses should include some direct mention of what the religious education team intends to do to help the person become qualified.

The successful recruiter will listen carefully to such objections for indications of hidden or underlying meanings. Gentle probing may bring these to the surface. Often the potential recruit is, in actuality, making a statement of self-image. Moses made just such a statement before the burning bush Recruiter in Exodus 3:11. God's answer makes it clear that Moses had not been called in response to his abilities, but in order that he might be given the *opportunity* to participate in the unfolding plan of the Eternal. Moses' lack of ability was compensated by God's empowering for the task.

Steve McCurley and Sue Vineyard recommend that objections to volunteerism be answered and removed, though without dishonesty or becoming judgmental of others. It may help to categorize the objection. For example, if the objection is based upon false information, provide data to the contrary. If doubt is central to the objection, give evidence to affirm the value of the task. Addressing the immediacy of the need may help the person who stalls. Gentle coaxing may help the vacillating person. If a genuine difficulty is objected to, admit the problem, accept the criticism, but minimize the objection to the degree possible.

McCurley and Vineyard emphasize the importance of communicating urgency. The benefits of volunteering should be underscored; they receive as well as give. They may acquire valuable experience and gain skills through doing the task and receiving instruction. Emphasize the support to be given by coordinators and other religious educators. Yet arm twisting should be avoided; decisions under pressure will probably result in unhappiness for all involved. A second appointment might be scheduled, in which the potential volunteer can commit themselves to the task, possibly by telephone.

It may help at this point to emphasize that involvement in volunteering should not be compared with the commitment of taking a job. McCurley and Vineyard note that there are degrees of involvement in volunteer efforts; volunteers may be involved:

- openly -or- in secret
- by participating -or- just observing
- regularly -or- intermittently
- within the organization (a member) -or- outside it (nonmember)
- by confronting problems -or- working within them
- on a completely unpaid basis -or- be reimbursed for expenses
- purely to help others -or- to help self while helping others
- informally -or- more formally
- when asked -or- when the volunteer desires

Who Will Commit Themselves?

Fred Wilson conducted research specifically with Baby Boomers (ages thirty to forty-five at the time of his study) to identify the factors that distinguished those who volunteered for church ministry from those who did not. While his study is probably the best in this area, the findings are tentative as they reflect research of only four churches in Southern California. However, he states that his sample is probably representative of Baby Boomers in general.

While those who volunteered tended to see every Christian as called to service and their becoming involved in volunteer work as a gradual process, nonvolunteers in these churches emphasized the need for a special call to ministry (thus providing an excuse for their noninvolvement).

Fred Wilson sees the general call to service as more biblical, and thus leaders need to teach that every Christian is called to ministry. In addition leaders can help prospective volunteers link ministry opportunities with their own natural abilities, not a special calling. Spiritual gift inventories and other evaluations of abilities may help encourage nonvolunteers to become involved (see chapter nine). Furthermore, since involvement tends to be a gradual process for volunteers, he encourages volunteer recruiters to ask prospects to pray about it and check later for their response, rather than pressing for an immediate decision.

Fred Wilson's research also found that active volunteers:

1. Perceived their talents being used profitably
2. Found stimulation and fulfillment through volunteering
3. Were encouraged to be involved by family and friends

Curiously, those not involved in volunteer ministry tended to express a higher interest in the social needs of people and society and often felt that ministry is done out of obligation or duty. This would suggest that the three factors emphasized by active volunteers need to be emphasized by church leaders. However, the key to activating those not currently involved may be to address their distinctive concerns.

Sometimes those who do not volunteer actually want to help others but at the level of people's deepest needs. Wilson believes that leaders need to consider ways that can help them move toward accomplishing Baby Boomers' idealistic dreams of youth (during the 1960s and early 1970s) through volunteerism. The uninvolved may greatly desire that the church be involved in the social and personal suffering of individuals, and leaders that are open to developing new varieties of service in these areas are more likely to get these people involved. Wilson also believes that the church may have overemphasized duty and obligation, which in effect makes the noninvolved more resistant to volunteer involvement.

Church people who are uninvolved in volunteer work expressed an intense desire to study theology and other intellectual issues, perhaps reflecting a perceived lack of adequate training for volunteer ministry. This suggests that they need to examine their faith in detail, emphasizing lived faith rather than abstract, detached theology. Perhaps "spiritual mentors" can help them with religious matters in the context of volunteer work. Telling them they will receive both preservice and inservice training in religion may also help. (Religion, that is, learning to live out one's faith, takes priority over theology in the best training — see chapter four.)

Wilson also discovered that these individuals were unlikely to become involved because of exciting, personal testimonies of others. Perhaps this was because the testimonies were unconvincing or perhaps they heard complaints rather than joyous testimonies from volunteers. Clearly the individual reasons for noninvolvement can vary from person to person, and it is important that volunteer recruiters take these into account rather than base recruitment strategies on what the recruiter or others think is important. This includes an assessment of the individual's needs and linking needs to the volunteer task. For example:

1. Those who are oriented toward achievement may seek personal fulfillment and responsibility.

2. Those who want to be with others are more likely to respond to encouragement to participate and religious education tasks that attempt to meet the personal needs of others.

3. Those who are oriented toward status will prefer some degree of authority and leadership.

4. Those who are duty or guilt oriented may need to sense an obligation to serve (again, this is often overemphasized to the detriment of recruitment).

Another aspect of volunteer commitment considered by Wilson was the possible relationship between spiritual maturity and whether or not the person became a volunteer. Using Ellison's Spiritual Maturity Index Scale, he found no general relationship between spiritual maturity and volunteer involvement (perhaps this indicates a lack of spiritual mentorship at present). However, he did find a significant relationship between not being active in volunteer ministry and several items on the test. Specifically the noninvolved felt they needed "to take care of their own needs before they could serve" (the exact wording of the item). This may reflect concerns related to life transition issues, such as career, marriage, and/or family issues (e.g., caring for elderly parents, rearing teens). This suggests that a "no" to volunteer involvement should not be taken as unchangeable; as transitions occur they may change their priorities and come to a different decision. Again, it is important to encourage them to think and pray about an opportunity so they will decide gradually.

Nonvolunteers may also be wrestling with difficulties maintaining a regular devotional life or inability to resist temptations. Wilson suggests they would then require personal help in these areas before they are able to volunteer. Volunteer coordinators need to develop a sensitivity to those who feel they are unable to serve, or who feel they need a "vacation" from ministry. More pressure to volunteer may push them away from the church rather than get them more involved.

Who is most likely to make a commitment? Wilson gives us some valuable, research-based guidelines in this area, as well as suggestions for reaching those who are less likely to commit themselves. Certainly the climate and motivational atmosphere of the volunteer organization are also crucial elements in fostering commitment, which will receive attention throughout this book. McCurley and Vineyard underscore the fact that those who have talked to satisfied volunteers in the organization are more likely to get involved. "Nothing sells like a satisfied customer." Those who coordinate the volunteer religious education program might encourage ongoing volunteers to locate willing people for needed areas. The best "recruiters" are those who are happy about their own volunteer experiences.

For Further Reading

Ilsley, Paul, and John Niemi. *Recruiting and Training Volunteers*. New York: McGraw-Hill, 1981.

McCurley, Steve, and Sue Vineyard. *101 Tips for Volunteer Recruitment*. Downers Grove, Ill.: Heritage Arts, 1988.

Wilson, Fred. "Recruiting the Baby Boomer for Ministry." *Christian Education Journal* 11 (1990), pp. 51-68.

Part IV

Supervising and Training
Religious Education Volunteers

Chapter Twelve

Supervising and Orienting Volunteers to the Task

Once the volunteer is committed to the task at hand, initial orientation and training become priorities. Before they can effectively participate in religious education endeavors it must be ascertained that the individual possesses all the necessary skills required, as well as a working knowledge of how the religious organization functions.

Supervision

Orientation is one aspect of supervision in religious education. Supervision also includes inservice training of volunteers, evaluating the quality of the teaching that results, and encouraging improvement. Each of these supervisory functions is given a separate chapter in this book because they are so crucial to religious education success. The supervisor, a master teacher, works hand in hand with paraprofessionals and subprofessionals to instill high quality methods of teaching at all levels of the religious educator lattice.

The supervisor is *not* a manager or administrator of the religious education program. Administration is the job of the Director of Religious Education, who generally holds a position above the supervisor. Ken Gangel compares the religious education administrator to a business executive who runs a corporation, and the supervisor to a foreman. Commonly, CCD coordinators/directors or departmental/Sunday school superintendents do the supervision of volunteer religious educators, while the Director of Religious Education administers the programs of the church or organization. Both the supervisor and the DRE are professional, paid positions in many churches, although these two separate and distinct roles may be performed by a single person in the small church (see

Nancy Foltz' fine work on small churches). There may also be some variations in these roles and their positions in the church structure by denomination and possibly location (see Donald Rogers' work on urban churches). But even in exceptional cases, the DRE must maintain a clear-cut distinction between these two functions and work toward the addition of one or more separate professional religious education supervisor/s as soon as feasible.

Organizational administration *is* very important in religious education volunteerism, and later chapters of this book will consider administration in detail (see chapters nineteen to twenty-three). Certain aspects of administration may also prove to be helpful in supervision as well, including communicating (chapter twenty-two) and solving volunteer problems (chapter twenty-three). While supervisors can profit from the chapters on administration, the clear distinction between supervision and administration must be maintained (see David Bickimer's book on religious education leadership).

Orientation

In the orientation phase, the person gets to know the others in the program. In large churches they may have never met those they are to work with, and thus it is important for them to become acquainted. An initial orientation meeting and perhaps even a party or banquet can provide a means of introduction, perhaps in an informal context.

The orientation phase also includes learning how an organization operates. Many religious organizations (even some small churches) have developed manuals that state procedures and policies for distribution to volunteers. In some smaller groups these may be informally understood by long-term participants, but it is crucial that new volunteers come to understand these guidelines for the program. Writing them down prior to orientation of volunteers can ensure that the communication of these is accurate and complete, and may itself prompt more complete reflection upon what is best for the organizational process.

Responsibilities and methods of following up on the accomplishment of those responsibilities should also be included in the orientation. This includes attendance procedures, curriculum materials, amount of preparation expected, dress and other normative details, and so on. The more information, the better — unless the details become so numerous as to overwhelm the volunteer. If a great many details need to be included, a booklet is probably required.

Orientation can be provided independently, on a one-to-one basis, or in a large or small group context. Sometimes a combination of these approaches works best. Whatever approach is chosen, there is a trade-off of intimacy and efficiency. It is crucial for volunteers to be able to ask questions and share their concerns as part of the preparation process.

One of the writers of this book discovered the importance of orientation when he spent several months working for a small mission agency. No real orientation to the organization occurred prior to going overseas. When the author requested a set of policies and procedures, the directors of the mission agency stated that there was no current booklet of this nature. Once overseas, however, one of the directors began to set down oppressive regulations for those serving the mission organization, which produced a great deal of conflict and emotional turmoil. Eventually nearly every person on that particular field resigned. Much of the blame rests upon a lack of regulations and guidelines being presented and discussed prior to the overseas experience.

Preservice Training

Preservice instruction involves assessment of the capabilities of volunteers and equipping them with needed skills. While it is unlikely that a simple preservice program can produce skilled teachers from those who never have been involved in religious education previously, it may be possible to develop a minimally adequate educator through several preservice sessions. This minimal level of adequacy should then be advanced by regular, ongoing inservice sessions (see chapter thirteen). The best form of education occurs where there are training sessions interspersed with opportunities to practice what has been learned.

Eileen Starr recommends that the gender differences in motivation be taken into account by developing training programs that encourage distinct teaching styles oriented toward the needs of volunteers. Volunteer trainers should expect men to emphasize goal-setting and measurable results, while women can be expected to concentrate upon personal sharing and developing relationships. Most volunteers can be expected to have some spiritually based motivation, although Starr suggests that servanthood be emphasized in all training since spiritual altruism is not the highest motivation for most people. The distinct motivations each religious educator brings to volunteerism should be accepted, while spiritual altruism should particularly be nurtured.

Preservice training emphasizes the learning of skills needed for basic competence in the volunteer task. The degree of skill required relates directly to the goals and objectives of the program and the subsequent job description for the open position on the religious education lattice (see chapter four). Two important methods, modeling and shaping, are generally appropriate for preservice training.

Modeling involves the presentation of the desired behavior by another person for imitation by the new volunteer. This presentation may involve a live demonstration or a videotape of the activity (sometimes a cassette may be sufficient). The important thing is that the new volunteer observe the skills desired and then be given an opportunity to imitate. Research by Neal Chalofsky and Ralph Bates clearly indicates that modeling helps develop appropriate normative behavior in volunteer groups.

It is crucial that the demonstration emphasize key aspects of the task. One can watch a successful presentation, yet overlook the central reasons for that success. Someone who has considerable expertise can stop the demonstration temporarily at key points to emphasize crucial details. Videotapes may be paused for this emphasis as well. Key aspects of the skill to be learned might also be emphasized by charts and key terms presented by an overhead, a list handed out, exaggeration within the presentation, or captions over the picture on a videotape. What is most important, however, is that the action be stopped for the description and any possible questions or discussion that may ensue.

After a good model has been observed, the volunteer needs to be given the opportunity to imitate what has occurred in a realistic context. For example, if the task to be learned is telling children a story, the new volunteer should be given this opportunity. Surroundings should be as realistic as possible, including any needed visuals. Initial modeling might be one-to-one with a volunteer coordinator, to maximize immediate feedback and likelihood of success. Later an audience (perhaps an audience of peers who have been instructed to role-play being children) can be added. In the group learning context feedback might be deferred until after the entire sequence of desired behaviors involved in the given skill. Videotaping and replaying the volunteer's imitation can also be instructive. Specific behavior-by-behavior listing and analysis may be helpful using tools such as the Flanders scale (see chapter fourteen) or more simplified tabulations. James Michael Lee recommends that making even the simple distinctions between cognitive, affective, and lifestyle content, tabulated in short intervals of a few seconds, can help the volunteer become more aware of their instructional behaviors and needs for correction.

Shaping. Not all aspects of the volunteer's task should be learned at one time. It is important to break down the job description into component parts for learning singly at first, then combining them once the component skills have been learned. Indeed one can make a case for using shaping throughout the volunteer process: It begins with sensitizing and informing people as to needs, followed by commitment and support for that commitment. The third step is observation and involvement. Finally the volunteer begins to convince others of the need for involvement.

Shaping refers to the gradual acquisition of a skill in successive stages. Psychologists can teach rats to press a bar to acquire food. Human beings likewise are motivated, either by internal or external consequences of their behavior, as has been emphasized in several other sections of this book. Here we are emphasizing not the motivation, but rather the sequence of skills in learning the task. At first psychologists give the animal food when the rat only looks in the direction of the bar. When the animal has acquired this aspect of the task, psychologists stop rewarding this behavior and require the rat to move toward the bar to get the reward. Eventually the animal stays near the bar regularly. At this point the reward ceases for this behavior and the rat is required to stand on its hind legs near the bar to get the reward. Eventually, step by step, the animal comes to press the bar with its paws to obtain the reward. The greatest significance of this sequence of learning is that the rat is very unlikely to press a bar by accident — but through systematic shaping this behavior is acquired.

How can volunteers be shaped? Assuming they are highly motivated to learn the desired skill (see the sections on motivation in chapters nine, eleven, fifteen, and seventeen), emphasis must be placed on accurate assessment of skill components, giving the results of that assessment, and suggestions for improvement. Shaping implies that perfect skill performance is not the initial goal, but rather learning at least one new aspect of the skill.

For example, following the earlier example of storytelling, one of the first skills to be developed would be using an expressive voice. The new volunteer would listen to an expert storyteller go through a story (or part of a story), while key aspects of inflection, rate, and volume are highlighted. Then the new volunteer would be given the opportunity to model this aspect of storytelling and be provided with direct feedback on progress. Additional opportunities for imitation would be provided if the skill has not adequately been acquired. The accomplished storyteller (either in person or by videotape) might need to repeat the imitated performance if the key details need reiteration.

After adequate inflection, rate, and volume have been learned, another aspect of the presentation needs to be highlighted, such as hand movements, eye contact, and other body language accompanying the story. While these are being learned, the volunteer may need corrective feedback if they forget to include the previously learned aspects of the presentation. A third component of storytelling, use of visuals such as a flannelgraph, puppets, or other illustrative material, would be the third step in shaping storytelling skills to children. Each of the above three components may need to be broken down into finer details if the new volunteer has never told stories to children previously.

It is imperative that the instructor of new volunteers be well acquainted with the components needed to be effective in the volunteer's role. In most cases they should not only know those components but also be able to perform them so that on-the-spot modeling by example can be given. In the next chapter we will emphasize the importance of the mentor in learning religious education skills by volunteers.

Microteaching. James Michael Lee describes microteaching as a teaching context in which the skills needed are "telescoped" into a single teaching unit. Lee suggests nine steps in the microteaching process:

1) Identifying the skills needed
2) Observing videotaped presentations of the skill by a master teacher
3) The volunteer develops a short lesson which involves the use of the above skill
4) The volunteer presents that lesson to a small group within a shortened time period
5) A videotape of the presentation is played and analyzed by both the volunteer and the supervisor, underscoring both those places where the skill to be learned is practiced and when it was not appropriately practiced
6) The volunteer then plans the minilesson once again in such a manner that the desired skill will be included more consistently
7) The volunteer teaches this new lesson to a similar group of learners
8) A videotape of this second lesson is analyzed by the volunteer and his or her supervisor
9) The above sequence of revising the lesson, playing the videotape, and analysis is repeated until the skill is mastered

James Michael Lee also encourages the use of reflective methods as a necessary adjunct to microteaching. Again, the use of the Flanders system and behavior analysis approaches to analyze activities is valuable, but active reflection *during* teaching is a necessary complement to coding techniques.

Placement

Following orientation and preservice instruction volunteers should be placed as quickly as possible. Lengthy waiting times will undercut motivation and interest. Indeed one can make a case that orientation and preservice sessions that are planned for volunteers when there are no openings in those areas are a waste of time. In most religious education contexts placement must *follow* at least some minimal orientation and preservice instruction, not precede them or occur simultaneously, as often happens in churches and organizations desperate for help. It may prove preferable to go without a program for a period of time and then begin that program with adequately prepared people, than to begin with poorly prepared volunteers.

Placement must coincide primarily with the competencies and interests of the volunteer and secondarily according to the needs of the church or parachurch organization. This is an important emphasis in light of the recent trends in volunteerism, which appear to hold true in religious contexts as well. Burnout occurs more often when placement is primarily done on the basis of the organization rather than the volunteer.

Placement includes specifying the amount of time committed to volunteering. Open-ended volunteer service is largely a thing of the past. Most people in today's society prefer limited time commitments, which can be renewed if all involved are pleased with the results. Short commitments are more likely to be made than long commitments, thus the religious group should probably consider quarterly commitments (or less in some circumstances) rather than yearly commitments as in the past.

Sometimes when the volunteer has negative past experiences or limited training that cause directors to have some doubt about the likelihood of successful performance, probationary placement can occur. Conversely, probation may be a necessary element in situations that for some reason have inadequate training programs or when the task can only be defined vaguely.

Orienting volunteers to the task involves general orientation, preservice training, and proper placement. But this is not the end of training for the volunteer. Regular, ongoing inservice training is also important, a topic to be considered in detail in the next chapter.

For Further Reading

Bickimer, David A. *Leadership in Religious Education*. Birmingham, Ala.: Religious Education Press, 1989.

Chalofsky, Neal, and Ralph Bates. "Using Group Process Techniques to Increase Task Force Effectiveness: A Case Study." *Journal for Specialists in Group Work* 9 (May 1984), pp. 93-98.

Foltz, Nancy T. *Religious Education in the Small Membership Church*. Birmingham, Ala.: Religious Education Press, 1990.

Gangel, Kenneth. *Leadership in Religious Education*. Chicago: Moody, 1970.

Lee, James Michael. "How to teach: Foundations, Processes, Procedures." In *Handbook of Preschool Religious Education*, ed. Donald Ratcliff, pp. 152-216. Birmingham, Ala.: Religious Education Press, 1988.

Roadcup, David. *Recruiting, Training, and Developing Volunteer Youth Workers*. Cincinnati, Ohio: Standard, 1987.

Rogers, Donald B. *Urban Church Education*. Birmingham, Ala.: Religious Education Press, 1989.

Schindler-Rainman, Eva, and Ronald Lippitt. *The Volunteer Community*, 2nd ed. La Jolla, Calif.: University Associates, 1977.

Starr, Eileen. *A Description of the Motivations for Teaching Identified by Lay Volunteer Sunday School Teachers*. Ed.D. dissertation, Deerfield, Ill.: Trinity Evangelical Divinity School, 1989.

Chapter Thirteen

Training Volunteers as They Work

Education should be offered on a continuing basis for volunteers, usually termed "inservice" education. Continuing education may offer the volunteer a means to personal growth as well as a means of developing certain skills. Learning from experts, exchanging information with other volunteers, and overcoming problems in one's volunteer efforts become worthy goals of inservice instruction. Researcher George Barna notes that conveying the concept of personal growth as an outcome of volunteerism motivates participation, thus this aspect of training should be underscored regularly. Barna also notes that healthy, growing churches provide high quality guidance and inservice training. Likewise James Michael Lee provides ample research evidence that inservice training leads to quality religious education (we will examine Lee's approach in detail later in this chapter). Inhouse training as well as workshops, conferences, and other kinds of meetings can also help fulfill the training requirement, as can independent study approaches.

While the training techniques considered in the previous chapter can help in conducting effective inservice training, there are distinctive aspects to continuing education of volunteers. It is more likely that the instructor will be building upon prior skills, producing enhanced performance rather than developing entirely new skills. In addition, when volunteers are already involved in volunteer service there is a greater likelihood they will bring to the training questions and a highly motivated desire to relate the training to the specific tasks required at their level of the religious educator lattice (see chapter four). The learning is less likely to be a sterile academic exercise and more likely to be perceived as task-relevant.

Who should do the training? It is generally conceded that the teacher needs to know more about the topic than the learner about the tasks at hand. However, one can also make a case that teachers need to point the learner to helpful resources as much as providing specific information themselves. One study by Frederick Seymour and Karyn France indicates that volunteers can learn to teach others (in this case, volunteers were taught to teach parents of behavior-disordered children management skills for use in the home). Instructing and helping teachers can itself be a volunteer position. In most religious education contexts, however, the religious education director or an experienced public school teacher, either of which involves professional expertise, provides this training.

Difficulties exist in scheduling inservice training. If training is provided in a group context, it may be wise to at least separate training groups by age of the learners involved. In other words, those who teach or are otherwise involved with children should probably be given inservice training separate from those who work with adults, because of the distinctive needs and characteristics of differing age groups, as well as different approaches and techniques used with each group. One church, however, substituted teacher training for a midweek service in which they built a Bible lesson around that week's Sunday school lesson, which was the same for all age levels. Age-specific applications were individualized for each age grouping, but the general theological and biblical exegesis was provided collectively. A combination of this approach and additional inservice training distinctive to the specific age level to be taught is a worthy possibility for churches. Another consideration would be possible separation by levels on the religious educator lattice.

Group instruction has the advantage of maximizing the inservice teachers' time, but that advantage comes at the cost of less convenience for the volunteers. In contrast, individualized instruction takes more of the inservice trainer's time but is more likely to be convenient for the volunteer. Sometimes videotapes or cassette recordings can make the scheduling more convenient (for example one can listen to a cassette while driving to and from work). Of course the disadvantage of these "canned" approaches stems from the greater difficulty getting feedback about specific problems in the religious education context or obtaining clarification about the inservice training. Perhaps a combination of approaches is ideal, with the most common method being recorded instruction, occasional group meetings for feedback, and possible individual feedback. (See James Michael Lee's work, cited at the end of this chapter, for more on the use of media in inservice training.)

Motivating Volunteers to Attend Training

What is it that motivates volunteers to be present at inservice sessions? In a study of Sunday school volunteers who attended a training convention in Los Angeles, reported by Fred Wilson, the highest motivating factor was the desire to help others grow spiritually ("ministry preparation"). Two other factors — the desire for personal spiritual growth and the desire for cognitive learning for its own sake — were also more significant than all other motives for attending the training sessions. The typical volunteer acted from a combination of motives, not just a single motivational factor.

In a somewhat similar study of motivation for attending training conducted with Roman Catholics, J. M. Utendorf found that personal religious development was the highest motivator. Somewhat less motivating, but still significant, were the desire to give service to church and community, and intellectual interest in the training.

A Search Institute study, reported by Eugene Roehlkepartain, similarly named Bible learning and improved teaching abilities as the top motivators for religious education volunteers who work with children. Wilson's study indicated that motivation to attend training did not differ significantly by gender. However, those who volunteered to work with children and preteens placed cognitive learning as a priority over spiritual growth as motivators. Volunteers who worked with young adults were less oriented toward ministry preparation, while religious education volunteers involved with middle and older adults were more motivated by the desire for spiritual growth than preparation.

Ethnic differences in motivation also surfaced in Wilson's research. Blacks listed cognitive learning as their top motivator for attending. Koreans listed the relationship with God as the second most important motivator. While in general there were no significant differences by church size, those who attended small churches (churches with less than a hundred) were far more likely to attend due to the desire for social contact.

The above research suggests that it is important to analyze the prospective inservice audience prior to conducting the training. Religious education volunteers may be less likely to attend training sessions if we do not appeal to what motivates them most effectively. Utendorf and Wilson provide us with important guidelines regarding this motivation, guidelines that may need expanding or revision according to specific church or religious education organization contexts.

Mentoring

In recent years the field of adult education has underscored the importance of mentoring relationships. This involves a close relationship between a highly skilled, experienced individual and the less experienced learner. The teacher-student status differences are deemphasized, while partnership is highlighted. In the context of religious education, this may be a partnership between a master teacher and the newer, less experienced teacher. Both mentor and learner spend time together dealing with problems and potential solutions, either within the religious education context, outside that context, or both. Research by Margaret Cellerino indicates that specialists can perform an invaluable role as mentor-advisors and even serve as critics at times within an educational context.

For example, a Sunday school teacher "taught" a class of nine-year-olds by simply reading the Sunday school booklet to them. As a result the children began throwing paper airplanes, running about the room, and showing considerable disrespect for the teacher. When the teacher asked for help, a retired school teacher was asked to "co-teach" the class. The two met together for several hours the day before the class, "brainstorming" ideas for visuals, games, and other group activities that would help in teaching the content more effectively. The next class session went far more successfully, but the original teacher asked that the retired school teacher continue to help with preparation the next Saturday. Again, they did some brainstorming, and the experienced teacher role-played telling a Bible story with exaggerated inflection and visuals. The new teacher imitated the role-play several times until she was able to do the story well. Regular feedback including encouragement and pointing out weak areas of the storytelling helped refine the technique. The next Sunday proved even more successful. The informal training continued for several weeks, during which the two became good friends. Eventually the new teacher agreed to try the lesson preparation and teaching on her own, with the master teacher observing and giving feedback after class. Again this met with success, so the newer teacher agreed to simply report the results of classes week by week, and only when problems arose would they get together for more planning or training.

Mentoring which includes learning through imitation (or modeling) can be considered the method most used by Jesus in his earthly ministry. His disciples learned to follow the example of their master teacher, although they obviously fell short of that model at times.

The Content of Instruction

James Michael Lee has developed a model of teaching religious educators which is equally relevant to the training of volunteers in this area. *The Flow of Religious Instruction* gives the fullest description of teaching teachers, while his more recent *The Content of Religious Instruction* emphasizes what is taught through religious education, and his first book of the trilogy *The Shape of Religious Instruction* best articulates his paradigm, or macrotheory, of social science as the basis for religious education. Lee has also given more brief treatments to these topics within the REP developmental books on religious education (listed at the end of this chapter).

Instruction always involves several different kinds of substantive contents (in contrast to structural content — the teaching act itself), some of which the educator may not even be aware. For example, there is "product content" which is the observable results produced by instruction. But, simultaneously, there is "process content" which is less observable but involves the way the learner accomplishes something. Thus how the student learns to live out faith is process content, while being able to list aspects of one's theology is product content.

Lee also mentions "verbal content," the words used in teaching, which contrasts with "nonverbal content," the tone, pitch, and tempo of voice, eye movements, facial expressions, gestures, and body language. All of these affirm or disconfirm the verbal message. When the verbal and nonverbal contents are inconsistent with one another, people usually trust the nonverbal.

Other contents mentioned by Lee include the conscious (the teacher is aware of it) and the unconscious. He also contrasts cognitive (mental) with affective (feeling-oriented) contents. Last of all, Lee considers lifestyle content, which involves the overall living out of one's religion. While all of the contents are important, the lifestyle is perhaps the most crucial because it is the result most likely to be observed in everyday life.

Lee tells a story from early in his teaching career that vividly portrays how the substantive (verbal and nonverbal) contents can diverge from the structural content (the teaching act) within the same individual at virtually the same point of time. He observed a visiting European professor gently, quietly telling a group of graduate students how they should teach children to love Jesus. When a few seminarians arrived late to the presentation, he turned to them and angrily denounced them for their tardiness. He ordered them to leave, and after they had departed he returned to his calm, gentle description of teaching children to love Jesus. The structural content of the professor's interaction with students vastly contradicted the verbal and nonverbal substantive content of his teaching. Many years later those students recall the pain of that interaction far better than any other aspect of the course.

The inservice trainer must help volunteers become aware of all these contents in their own teaching. The most effective teachers are aware, at least to some extent, of the different levels at which they teach. But, in addition, those who teach volunteers must also be aware of the contents which they teach and that the teaching act itself can negate what they are attempting to teach. As noted in the previous chapter, they provide important models of each of the above contents. This again underscores the importance of the teacher of volunteers being a master teacher, one that not only knows the content volunteers need to know, but also models an exemplary personal life and considers how that content is conveyed. It should also be noted that the structural content is a priority in interactions subprofessionals have with children, and indeed at all levels of the religious educator lattice.

Teaching Teachers to Teach

Lee emphasizes teaching as both a science and an art; both knowing and doing (see chapter four). Thus inservice instruction (as well as preservice training) must involve the practice of teaching in differing contexts, so that the art is refined. Likewise, volunteers need to learn theories behind specific techniques of religious education, theories based upon good research, so that the science of teaching affects the educator's behavior. The art and science of good teaching combine with, and help produce, appropriate techniques essential to quality instruction.

Sometimes inexperienced volunteers (and too often even experienced professionals) may fail to appreciate the holistic aspect of religious instruction. They may view education as simply something conveyed to the learner. Religious education, as an art and a science, includes the importance of feedback from the student to the teacher which provides information both about what the student is learning and the effectiveness of the instruction. This feedback gives an informed basis for the teacher changing his or her approach in light of the results of the teaching. Thus the teacher's instruction is a behavior which initiates the student's behavior, which in turn initiates a subsequent teacher behavior (refinement of the instructional event or moving on to another instructional event), which then initiates another student behavior, and so on. The chain of events is a unit in which student and teacher are both acting and reacting (see Weick's concept of "cycles" in chapter seven for an interesting parallel). The above process assumes the volunteer is teaching reflectively, analyzing the teaching activity and the results, and thus becoming more aware of what actually occurs during instruction. Volunteers need to learn reflective teaching, both through formal instruction and perhaps through modeling by the instructor of the volunteers (e.g., through examples from their own teaching and even by conveying their reflection on teaching to the volunteers).

Training religious education volunteers involves helping them accomplish the goals that have been prescribed (see chapter six). The objectives of the religious instruction need to have been clearly defined in advance so that the volunteer will observe whether they have met those objectives. Inservice instruction may possibly involve teaching volunteers how to develop objectives within the more general goals and mission statement of the religious organization. The volunteer needs to at least partially comprehend how the overall philosophy of religious education, the mission statement of the organization, and the objectives all relate to the curriculum provided and the instruction they are to accomplish or help accomplish.

Evaluation and Training

As implied above, it is imperative that inservice training be, at least in part, clearly related to the evaluation of the volunteer's performance. Generic, nonspecific inservice training is more likely to be a hit-and-miss affair. This may have benefit as far as gaining general perspectives, introducing innovative techniques, or even producing motivation. However, specific feedback from the teacher's performance may indicate specific needs for inservice training. This feedback comes from the analysis of contents and teacher behavior, as well as reflective activities, all mentioned earlier in the previous chapter. As noted earlier, ideally this could be presented one-to-one by a master teacher, but recordings that deal with specific problems could also be used. What is crucial is that, in some way, specific feedback about the volunteer's work is provided, and —if needed— remedial instruction is given. The teacher performance center, described by James Michael Lee, is also an invaluable means to improvement (more on this in chapter fourteen). In this chapter we touched on the importance of feedback, a topic considered in detail in the next chapter.

For Further Reading

Barna, George. *User-Friendly Churches*. Ventura, Calif.: Regal, 1991.

Callerino, Margaret. "A Mentor-Volunteer Program for the Gifted and Talented." *Roeper-Review* 6:1 (1983), pp. 45-46.

Lee, James Michael. *The Shape of Religious Instruction* (1971); *The Flow of Religious Instruction* (1973); *The Content of Religious Instruction* (1985). Birmingham, Ala.: Religious Education Press.

Lee, James Michael. "How to Teach: Foundations, Processes, Procedures." In *Handbook of Preschool Religious Education*, ed. Donald Ratcliff, pp. 152-216. Birmingham, Ala.: Religious Education Press, 1988.

Lee, James Michael. "Procedures in the Religious Education of Adolescents." In *Handbook of Youth Ministry*, ed. Donald Ratcliff and James A. Davies, pp. 214-251. Birmingham, Ala.: Religious Education Press, 1991.

Lee, James Michael. "General Procedures of Teaching Religion." In *Handbook of Children's Religious Education*, ed. Donald Ratcliff, pp. 164-199. Birmingham, Ala.: Religious Education Press, 1992.

Roehlkepartain, Eugene. Olympic Style Volunteer Training. *Children's Ministry* 2:4 (1992), pp. 10-12.

Seymour, Frederick, and Karyn France. *Volunteers as teachers of child management to parents of behaviour-disordered preschoolers*. Leslie Center, Auckland, New Zealand: Presbyterian Social Service Association, 1984.

Utendorf, J. M. "Reasons for Participation in Roman Catholic Lay Ministry Training Programs." *Review of Religious Research* 26:3 (1985), pp. 281-292.

Wilson, Fred. "Why Church Volunteers Attend Religious Training Programs." *Christian Education Journal* 12:3 (1992), pp. 69-85.

Chapter Fourteen

Evaluating Volunteers' Work

The term "evaluation" may sound cold and mechanical to many, but the process is a key to effective programs. It is also an important biblical concept. Charles Foster reminds us that Nathan evaluated King David regarding his adultery and murder. Thus evaluation (in this case the evaluation of faulty values, while in religious education the evaluation of instruction) becomes the basis for confession of failure to live up to ideals and subsequent efforts toward improvement. Also recall Jesus' statement, "By the fruits of their labors shall you know them," which also assumes evaluation is a necessity.

Foster offers the following guidelines for evaluation:

1. Evaluation should include everyone in the learning context, both the learners and the religious education volunteers (at all levels of the religious educator lattice — see chapter four).

2. Check information given in the evaluation for accuracy (more than one evaluator or evaluation helps establish reliability).

3. Make sure the standards for the evaluation are known to everyone.

4. Use the evaluation to improve teaching and learning (and other activities appropriate to the level of the religious educator lattice).

5. Be sure the method of evaluation relates to the objectives of the lesson — accomplishing the intended goals must be the priority.

It is also important to use a variety of evaluation methods, both formal and informal, directive (questionnaires with options to choose from) and nondirective (open-ended questions). This is important in the testing of students for what they have learned as well as the evaluation of religious educator effectiveness.

Marlene Wilson reminds us that evaluation relates directly to planning. The objectives and standards that have been set for meeting those

129

objectives are the focus of the evaluation process. Evaluation of other areas may help explain why those objectives are —or are not— being met, yet the initially planned mission of the group and objectives of the specific area of religious education must be primary in the evaluation. In other words, the most important question is, "Are the objectives being met?"

Evaluation should occur not only during natural pauses in the rhythm of the religious education cycle (i.e., at the end of a curriculum unit), but also on an ongoing basis within those cycles. Evaluation of the students and volunteers should be differentiated from the evaluation of the program, to be considered in chapter twenty-four. The program evaluation considers the overall effectiveness of the organization's volunteer program, while volunteer evaluation considers the individual volunteer's effectiveness, and student evaluation considers specific learning outcomes.

The remainder of this chapter will concentrate upon the formative evaluation of the volunteer (evaluation for the purpose of improvement), yet it must be emphasized that volunteers learning to evaluate students is a priority, particularly at higher levels of the religious educator lattice. For more details on evaluating learning, see the chapter by David Starks and Donald Ratcliff listed at the end of this chapter.

What are some of the things about volunteers to be evaluated? Mark Senter suggests eight areas to be considered:

1. The characteristics of the teacher/s and other religious educators. This includes how friendly, enthusiastic, and open they are with students.

2. The adequacy of preparation. Did the religious educator arrive on time, was the learning environment attractive, was the lesson prepared adequately?

3. What methods were used? A list of methods might be stated so the evaluator can circle those that occurred. The evaluator might also comment on whether the methods were appropriate to the lesson and the skill with which methods were used.

4. The degree of teamwork between teachers and/or assistants (as well as others on the religious educator lattice). Did they cooperate, was discipline adequate but not excessive, and were the religious educators organized?

5. Lesson content. Was the lesson theologically and biblically sound, did the instruction represent mastery of the content, and were practical applications made?

6. Participation by learners. Did they become involved during the

beginning activities and all subsequent instruction? Was there a difference in participation between large and small group settings?

7. Was there evidence of lesson impact? What was accomplished and what evidence is there for that accomplishment?

8. Summary of strengths, weaknesses, and suggestions for improvement.

Attendance patterns of teachers, assistants, other religious educators, and students certainly warrant consideration. A pattern of nonattendance or being late by any of these may indicate a difficulty that needs to be investigated. The productiveness of the person should also be considered. Do they use their time wisely and efficiently? Do they accomplish the goals and objectives of the unit or job description? The relationship between the volunteer and peers or administrators is also a factor for evaluation.

Assessment of Teaching Skills by the Organization

While many of the above aspects of volunteer work can be evaluated through checklists, informal questioning, and casual observation, the effectiveness of specific instructional behavior is often more difficult to assess. James Michael Lee has suggested that churches and other religious organizations develop teacher performance centers to more accurately assess and train effective teaching. Such a center is a "concrete pedagogical laboratory" in which the behaviors involved in teaching are recorded in some manner (usually videotape) and then analyzed by the teacher either by himself or herself, or with a supervisor. As a result the teacher learns to sharpen teaching competence by changing pedagogy. Lee believes that providing such a laboratory may be the most significant thing any religious organization can do to maximize the quality of instruction provided. If the individual church is unable to develop such a laboratory he suggests that several churches, probably within the same denomination and in close proximity, might share a common laboratory. Certainly seminaries might develop such laboratories and make them available to nearby churches as well as use them in training seminarians. Again, the emphasis is upon formative evaluation to improve religious education abilities.

Lee also advocates using teacher assessment tools, such as the Flanders Interaction Analysis System. This device breaks down teacher behavior into ten categories:

1. Acceptance of feelings
2. Encouraging or praising

3. Using or accepting student ideas
4. Asking a question
5. Lecture
6. Providing directions
7. Justifying or criticizing of authority
8. Students responding by talking
9. Student initiates by talking
10. Confusion or silence

The goal of the Flanders system is to be *nonjudgmental* — these are categories of behavior, not value-laden scales of right and wrong. Values can certainly be brought to bear on the results of the evaluation, but they are not inherent in the scale itself. Some have pointed out the weakness of the scale in the limited evaluation of student activity, but others view this as a strength in that evaluating the teacher is the prime consideration. Lee cites the work of Raymond Whiteman as strong evidence that the Flanders evaluation can be successfully used in religious education contexts. When combined with high quality feedback from the supervisor, improvement in teacher behavior is likely.

As mentioned in an earlier chapter, Lee has also used a three-category system to assess teaching. The categories —cognitive, affective, and lifestyle— are itemized every five to eight seconds as a teacher watches a videotape of his or her own teaching. The resulting profile of teaching will indicate any imbalances in these content areas. Evaluation need not be complex.

Mark Senter notes that sometimes religious education volunteers can become self-conscious of professionals evaluating their performance. He recommends the following guidelines for evaluations by leaders:

1. Notify teachers (and other religious educators) two weeks prior to the evaluation.
2. Evaluate for three weeks in a row so that a complete view of what is occurring will be obtained.
3. The evaluator should arrive well before the beginning of the instructional session and not leave until the session has ended.
4. The evaluator should stay in the area so religious educators can discuss some aspects of what occurred, although detailed discussion of the evaluator's findings should not occur until later.
5. The evaluator should use a standard evaluation form with which the instructors are acquainted.
6. The evaluator should be careful not to intrude upon the instruction in any way (see Lofland and Lofland for guidelines).

7. Religious educators and the evaluator should meet together to discuss the results within two weeks after the final observation.

Assessment by Learners

Learners should also participate in the assessment of religious instruction. Such assessments have become virtually universal in higher education, so that learner satisfaction and areas that might be overlooked in supervisory evaluation can be ascertained.

Certainly learner evaluation is far from objective. Learners who personally like a teacher or other religious educator tend to rate them high on all scales and perhaps not give full attention to the different areas they are to evaluate (called "the halo effect"). The opposite can also occur. Sometimes learners fail to take educator evaluation seriously and make random marks on the evaluations. The quality of such teacher evaluation scales also varies and sometimes a measurement instrument will not include measures of teacher behavior critical to the topic area (this would especially seem likely in religious education). Any measurement must allow plenty of room for learners to make their own qualitative comments about the religious educator's activities and not be merely rating scales. Even though such scales measure satisfaction more than anything else, this is an important measure in religious education endeavors.

Students might also be informally contacted by volunteer supervisors or other religious education administrators regarding the classroom activities. It is crucial that we not rely upon periodic visits to class alone to provide feedback, as teachers and other religious educators can and do modify their behavior in the presence of an evaluator. Likewise formal assessment tools filled out by learners may not capture nuances that can be obtained by informal discussions with those learners regarding the volunteer's behavior.

Assessment by Co-workers or Guests

George Barna, in his study of churches that are growing numerically and spiritually, notes that these churches seriously consider the evaluations made by guests at their churches as an important source of feedback. Brief assessments of religious education activities by guests may provide more of an outsider's view of what occurs. These can be important to increasing the popularity of the religious education efforts.

Co-workers may also be an important source of assessment information. While teacher assistants and others on the religious educator lattice can obviously give their impressions of religious educator behaviors, the professional religious educator can provide invaluable information about the activities of interns, assistants, and other religious education volunteers. All assessments, of course, must be weighed considering personal prejudices, individual values, personality factors, and other subjective components. Of course, this is true with any evaluation at any level.

As with organizational assessment, it is important to not be intrusive in the evaluation. Evaluators need training not only in the specific method of evaluation, but also in how to evaluate without intruding upon the ongoing religious education activities. Some good ideas in this regard can be found in the helpful little book titled *Analyzing Social Settings* by Lofland and Lofland.

Self-Assessment

Self-critique may also be involved, where the volunteer evaluates his or her own performance. There is, of course, the danger that the self-assessment will be filled out simply to please or impress supervisors. But, conscientiously and reflectively performed, self-assessment can be valuable for personal improvement.

Videotaping can aid self-assessment. While many people are self-conscious at first in front of the video camera, most eventually relax and may even forget its presence. One-way mirrors can also help make the video camera less intrusive for students. Afterward the instructor can replay the videotape to conduct self-assessment, perhaps combining this assessment with a peer or supervisor who also watches the videotape. The emphasis, again, is to be a nonjudgmental cooperative formative assessment, oriented toward improvement of competence.

Communicating the Assessment

The religious education director, or other director of volunteers, should accurately reflect upon both the strengths and weaknesses of volunteers. This is then followed by a discussion with the volunteer, usually one-to-one, of what has been observed. Constructive suggestions will help the volunteer see that the evaluation is of potential benefit for their own increased understanding and effectiveness.

Deficiencies in skill areas should be described as specific behaviors and form the basis for behavioral objectives for inservice training. Thus the results of evaluation directly feed back into a system of remedial instruction. To be of maximal value, these objectives can —when appropriate— be related to the mission of the religious organization. Evaluation of volunteers is an ongoing process, preferably to be done periodically during an instructional unit as well as at the conclusion of that unit.

Regardless of whether problems are skill-based or in other areas of the volunteer's behavior, he or she should be systematically and effectively encouraged to improve. This topic will be considered in detail in the next chapter.

For Further Reading

Barna, George. *The Frog and the Kettle*. Glendale, Calif.: Regal, 1990.

Foster, Charles. *The Ministry of the Volunteer Teacher*. Nashville: Abingdon, 1986.

Lee, James Michael. *The Flow of Religious Instruction*. Birmingham, Ala.: Religious Education Press, 1973.

Lofland, J., and L. Lofland. *Analyzing Social Settings*, 2nd ed. Belmont, Calif.: Wadsworth, 1984.

Senter III, Mark. *Recruiting Volunteers in the Church*, rev. ed. Wheaton, Ill.: Victor, 1990.

Starks, David and Donald Ratcliff. "Planning, Evaluation, and Research." In *Handbook of Preschool Religious Education*, ed. Donald Ratcliff, pp. 270-287. Birmingham, Ala.: Religious Education Press, 1988.

Whiteman, Raymond. *The Differing Patterns of Behavior as Observed in Teachers of Religion and Teachers of Mathematics and Social Studies*. Unpublished seminar project, Graduate Program in Religious Education, University of Notre Dame, 1971.

Wilson, Marlene. *The Effective Management of Volunteer Programs*. Boulder, Col.: Volunteer Management Associates, 1976.

Chapter Fifteen

Encouraging Volunteer Improvement

Improvement of volunteer task performance is a key goal for those who help direct religious education efforts. How can volunteers be encouraged to improve? While direct, though kind, evaluation and training usually proves the most effective, sometimes seminars, tape recordings, and other instructional means may be useful as well. These would require that the volunteer be very self-reflective, analyzing their religious education performance as they listen. But it is far too easy for people to apply content to the weaknesses of others rather than examine themselves.

Defense Mechanisms

Even when the person, at some level, becomes aware of weaknesses and difficulties (personally or in their educational performance), the unconscious mind can easily throw up one of many defenses to disguise the real weakness. For example, they can *project* the problem onto others — see it as originating from other people rather than themselves, or "pass the buck," so to speak. Or they may resort to *rationalization* by giving a socially acceptable reason for doing something rather than the real reason. Anger may be *displaced* upon someone other than the source of the problem. Or, under stress, the individual may *regress* to immature behavior. One of the more common defense mechanisms is *denial*, in which any difficulty pointed out by another person is simply denied.

For example, when a paraprofessional religious educator was confronted with the fact that the adults in her class complained they were not learning anything, she immediately blamed the complaints on poor curriculum and an assistant who missed one Sunday. The real difficulty, the paraprofessional spending only a half hour in preparation, was sidestepped. The blame had effectively been shifted to other sources.

Rationalization appeared in a Bible study leader who attracted fewer and fewer people to his class. When asked why the number had decreased from fifteen to five, he responded that there was a need to "prune" those who were not really spiritual from the group so that the rest could "get down to the business of spiritual living." In truth, people dropped out because they did not like the harsh, narrow sermons that had become dominant in the group sessions; the members of the group were being preached at instead of encouraged to participate.

A woman used displacement when she began yelling at the children in her after-service Sunday school class. The morning sermon caused her to be upset. She had unconsciously become angry at the pastor because he had given an illustration that was too much like an event in her life, but she would not admit that anger so she took it out on the kids. This could also happen at the subprofessional level of the religious educator lattice, such as a church bus driver displacing anger upon the riders.

One man, confronted with a weakness in his administration of a religious education program, rather than own up to that weakness, began to childishly make fun of the board members' names. He emotionally regressed to immature behavior because of the unconscious anxiety aroused by the confrontation.

The individual who can never admit to being wrong often uses the defense mechanism of denial to cover up mistakes. It is both mentally healthy, and a Christian virtue, to be open to criticism and reflect carefully upon that critique. In contrast, some have gotten into the habit of denying the possibility of error, thus cutting themselves off from significant personal and spiritual growth.

What can be done to overcome defense mechanisms? Psychodynamic psychology emphasizes the need to deal with the underlying anxiety behind those mechanisms. They are understood to be defending more basic underlying unconscious problems from early childhood and perhaps other more recent conflicts. Pointing out the possibility of defense mechanisms is likely to produce yet another defense mechanism (denial). While ideally counseling may help alleviate the dormant, unconscious anxiety, it may be that a volunteer coordinator can simply give a listening ear to the defensive person. Summarizing their statements in different words, accepting their hostility and fear, and providing an open receptivity to their ideas may decrease defensiveness. Sometimes psychological defensiveness reaches the extreme at which the individual cannot get along with others and the possibility of dismissal must be considered (see chapter eighteen). One might also consider the possibility of defense mechanisms as

simply habits that, if ignored, may decrease in frequency or stop altogether. On the other hand, defense mechanisms tend to be perpetuated if
they pay off in some way. For a more detailed analysis of defense mechanisms, see Paul Meier et al.

Some Possible Areas Needing Improvement

While defense mechanisms may keep the individual from accurately
understanding their weak areas and thus avoid improvement, there are
other more general difficulties that can emerge. The volunteer may
become bored, careless, or "burned out."

Boredom with a volunteer position usually results in drop outs eventually. What can be done to restimulate the bored volunteer? Possibilities
include:

1. *Increase the variety* of activities and tasks
2. *Increase responsibility*, if appropriate
3. *Increase the complexity* of the tasks to be accomplished
4. Consider the possibility of *evaluating* and *instructing other volunteers* (can be effective if it alleviates boredom, can make things
   worse if boredom gets passed on to others)
5. Encourage *library or action research* on improving skills
6. *Foster creativity* through books on the topic
7. *Change the curriculum*
8. Have them *evaluate different options* (such as curricula), giving
   positives and negatives of each possibility
9. *Assign a completely new task*

Not always, however, is boredom the problem. Sometimes carelessness
emerges in the performance of the activities required at the person's level
in the religious educator lattice. What can be done for the person who
becomes careless in performing the volunteer task? Here are some possibilities:

1. *Emphasize the mission and organizational objectives*, so they see the
   "big picture" more clearly.
2. Provide *more feedback* so they can see the quality of religious education is directly related to quality of results.
3. *Obtain their views on the organizational structure*, so they will be
   more personally involved and gain a sense of "ownership" of the task
   and organization.
4. *Encourage and reinforce* any aspects of the task that are done well.
   Break down the task into components, and rate each component on
   a scale from one to five.

5. Incompatibility with leaders and coworkers is a possibility, or there may simply be poor job fit at their level of the religious educator lattice — consider *alternative placement*.

6. May need more *recognition*.

Some volunteers become "burned out" because of overinvolvement either in the religious organization, or from overinvolvement with too many jobs in general. What can be done to help these individuals?

1. *Remove some of the responsibilities*.
2. Consider a *new assignment*.
3. *Increase variety* of activities and responsibilities.
4. *Provide "holidays"* when they are relieved from all responsibility of the task (more on this later in the chapter).
5. *Provide an assistant* or other paraprofessional to help.
6. *Point out that overinvolvement can easily produce burnout*.
7. *Confront compulsiveness*; help them realize absolute perfection is not only impossible, but may lead to burnout. For more on the subject of burnout, see chapter twenty-three.

Cognitive Dissonance

Social psychologist Leon Festinger has suggested that people often resolve mixed feelings by finding reasons for whatever they decide. For example, someone who buys a car often tries to remove doubts ("dissonance") about the decision by obtaining publicity literature supporting that decision. In other words, we try to remove self-doubts by finding confirming and reassuring reasons for the decision we made. We attempt to tip the scales in our direction so we will not feel as anxious (dissonant) about the decision. If this is impossible, we may relieve dissonance by changing behavior (e.g., buying a different car).

How does this relate to religious education volunteerism? We all tend to tell ourselves in various ways that we are doing well at our tasks; we look for evidence that confirms our self-confidence, so that dissonance will be minimal. But when religious education volunteers need to improve, it is necessary to point out weak areas and thus arouse dissonance so that a change in behavior will occur. The danger in the process is that the volunteer will decide it is not worth the effort and leave instead of change. Conversely, they may discount the need to change and simply ignore advice. The goal, then, is to arouse enough dissonance so that the person will change, but not so much that they leave. How can this be accomplished?

The key is to introduce dissonant information gradually, thus requiring some change in behavior. Too much dissonance is likely to result in avoidance (quitting the volunteer position). Too little dissonance is likely to result in self-justification ("I'm not that bad"). Areas of weakness and suggestions for correction need to be parceled out gradually, so that small but significant changes will occur. The result is analogous to shaping: gradual improvement occurs in the direction of the desired goal.

Bill was assigned to lead the young boys in the Trinity church recreational program. While the goal of the program involved helping develop good sportsmanship (a worthy goal for religious education), Bill himself sometimes fell short of that goal. He liked the boys, but sometimes poked fun at them when they made mistakes in playing softball. Bill's supervisor took him aside after a game and told him that he might consider giving the boys more encouragement when they played well. Bill responded that he already did that. Thereupon the supervisor more directly pointed out the teasing about mistakes might make some boys feel bad. Bill replied that he did not think this would be the case. Finally the supervisor mentioned a parent who had described an angry and upset son who did not show that anger on the field for fear of further ridicule from peers. The first comment by the supervisor might have been sufficient to correct some volunteers, but Bill did not see the personal implications for his behavior. Even the second comment that was more direct did not arouse sufficient dissonance to produce behavior change (though it might for most people). It was not until the scales were tipped in the other direction, through the specific example of the player who got angry at home from the teasing, that Bill was aroused to take action. He might very well change his behavior, or — if the dissonance was too high (and the rewards from volunteering too low) — he might stop coaching the church team. In addition this might only be one problem among others that Bill will eventually need to have pointed out and corrected. The rule of thumb is change one thing at a time and change it in manageable steps. For a more detailed analysis of dissonance theory, see Meier et al.

Recognition

Improvement is more likely when people receive reinforcement for past accomplishments. When an individual feels he or she has been adequately recognized for accomplishments, this tends to result in less defensiveness and greater motivation to do better. Volunteer coordinators need to look for positives in the volunteer's performance and give it attention and praise, so that they will be more receptive to negative feedback. The negative will more likely result in behavior change if accomplishment is rewarded.

William Bannon and Suzanne Donovan recommend a number of possible ways volunteers can be recognized:

1. List names of volunteers in bulletins, newsletters, and bulletin boards.

2. Plan a special service to recognize volunteers individually and collectively.

3. Give honors, certificates, and awards.

4. Reimburse costs incurred during volunteering.

5. Request the volunteer to publicly or privately report on their activities.

6. Send cards on birthdays, anniversaries, and other special times.

7. The provision of child care and good resources reinforces involvement. Inservice training might also be considered reinforcing for some.

8. Have special celebrations for the "volunteer of the month" and completion of special projects.

9. Banquets, dinners, and family picnics can be greatly appreciated, especially if the food is provided by others.

10. Additional responsibility is sometimes rewarding. Provide challenge.

11. Write recognition articles and volunteer-related news items for local newspapers.

12. Provide a party for volunteers.

13. Make surroundings pleasant at meetings and on the job.

14. Casually discuss their work with volunteers and thank them for their involvement. Give them time to individually talk with you.

15. Consider the development of support groups for volunteers where they can share their successes and joys.

16. Pass on compliments others give you for the volunteer's work.

17. Provide funds for workshops volunteers may attend.

18. Write notes of personal thanks.

19. Tell the volunteers' friends of their accomplishments.

20. Keep records of training and performance and offer to give them a positive reference for employment or additional ministries.

Planned Sabbaticals

Paul Maves emphasizes that planned leaves of absence from a volunteer position can also encourage volunteer improvement. Fatigue and burnout can occur when a person is too involved with any activity for too long. The commitment becomes a heavy obligation rather than something stimulating and interesting. Boredom and loss of interest can be alleviated sometimes by a lateral move to another, perhaps temporary position (say, helping in the fifth grade Sunday school instead of the seventh grade class for a quarter). Or it may be possible to simply program in a break after a given amount of time in a volunteer position. Observing other programs or areas of religious education in one's church (or possibly other churches) may enrich the "sabbatical," providing new insights and inspiration for the volunteer position. Enrolling in seminars may also prove helpful during the planned break in volunteer work. Finally, special projects may help fill the break time, such as curriculum development or a writing project.

For Further Reading

Bannon, William, and Suzanne Donovan. *Volunteers and Ministry*. New York: Paulist, 1983.

Festinger, Leon. *A Theory of Cognitive Dissonance*. Stanford, Calif.: Stanford University Press, 1957.

Maves, Paul B. *Older Volunteers in Church and Community*. Valley Forge, Pa.: Judson, 1981.

Meier, Paul, et al. *Introduction to Psychology and Counseling*. Grand Rapids, Mich.: Baker, 1991.

Part V

Drop-in and Drop-out
Religious Education Volunteers

Chapter Sixteen

Short-Term Volunteers

From Greek mythology comes the story of Narcissus, a very handsome young man, who reportedly had the wistful attention of all the young women in his village. He was, however, very aloof and proud. One day, Narcissus went hunting in the woods with some friends. Ultimately, he became separated from his companions and hopelessly lost.

Walking in the same woods was a young maiden by the name of Echo, who had a peculiar problem in that she could not formulate any words of her own. The only sound Echo could make involved immediately repeating what another said. Echo patiently watched from behind a tree and waited for Narcissus to speak.

Attempting to find his friends, Narcissus called out, "Where are you?"

"Where are you," Echo responded.

"Come to me," Narcissus pleaded.

"To me," came the Echo as she leaped from her hiding place. It might have ended a beautiful happily ever after love story, but for the pride of Narcissus. He spurned Echo's affection and left her alone to echo through the mountains.

Narcissus, on the other hand, wandered aimlessly for a time, finally discovering his reflection in a clear, still pool of water. As punishment, the gods caused him to fall in love with that reflection. Narcissus, according to the legend, became destined to love only himself from that point forward.

Today, strong evidence suggests that the spirit of Narcissus has been reborn in the Western world. Sociologists refer to the present age as the "me generation." The best-seller, *Looking Out for Number One*, epitomizes the narcissistic attitude that prevails, as does Christopher Lash's famous book *The Culture of Narcissism*. Two trends repeatedly appear in discussions of the present age which undoubtedly stem from the narcissistic tide.

Increased Time Demand

Baby boomers recall the amazement with which the West greeted the instant-on television. Waiting for tubes to warm was a thing of the past. "Instantaneous" became the buzz word of the day, which later ushered in automatic tellers, microwave ovens, all-night convenience stores, twenty-four hour news, fax machines, and overnight delivery.

Few people stopped to analyze the possibility that the instantaneous society served as a logical projection of narcissism. In the rush to self-gratification and "meism," it was reasoned, "my time is valuable to me." George Barna even suggests that by the year 2000 time could serve as currency, since it will hold more value than money.

Decreased Commitment

Barna also notes the increasing unwillingness to make long-term commitments as American society moves toward the year 2000. Evidences of the trend abound:
- The rising divorce rate
- Increasing acceptability of generic products indicating lack of brand loyalties
- Decreasing memberships in civic and fraternal organizations

The latter evidence appears to hold true even when membership involves a matter of principle. News reports in the early 1990s indicate that one of the co-founders of the very successful organization, Mothers Against Drunk Drivers (MADD) resigned in order to take a public relations position with a major producer of alcoholic beverages!

Perhaps the epitome of the decrease in commitment trend came recently when national media attention focused on a situation in which adoptive parents were attempting to undo the process of adoption, thereby divorcing a child of several years. The reporter of that event summarized with the label, "the uncommitted generation."

Business Response

Business and industry have felt the impact of these trends. A generation ago, employees typically held the same job throughout their productive years. Commonly, several generations worked for the same company or at the same profession. By contrast, today's work force changes jobs and professions frequently. The average household in America moves every six years, frequently for job-related reasons.

John Naisbitt and Patricia Aburdene suggest three business and industrial responses have grown out of these trends. These include: flextime, permanent part-time, and job sharing.

Flextime usually involves allowing employees to determine their starting and ending time, but not the total number of hours required. The total time required on the job may be computed weekly, monthly, or even annually. The cost of flextime to employers is very low, yet the benefits to employees are enormous. Industrial variations of flextime include four 10-hour, or even three 12-hour days.

While part-time work used to be associated with low skilled positions, increasingly, well-trained professionals choose the part-time option. The nursing profession has created a great number of these part-time positions in response to the tremendous need for employees. Even executives of major corporations today may be part-time.

The concept of job sharing grew out of the permanent part-time trend. In job sharing, two qualified employees share one full-time position. Many report that the balancing of skills and weaknesses, as well as schedules, creates a more agreeable situation for both the employee and the employer.

Religious Education Response

Short-term volunteerism in religious education parallels the business and industry response of flextime, permanent part-time, and job sharing. Many religious organizations are discovering that volunteers are willing to commit only for a briefer time frame than in the past. While many leaders find it tempting to sit back and wish for long-term help, cultural circumstances require adaptation.

As a result, many churches have moved toward CCD/Sunday school electives, especially in the adult curriculum. Teachers commit to teach an elective for a relatively short (perhaps a quarter) time frame. Students select an elective periodically, thus avoiding long-term commitment to an established Sunday school class.

Mission boards have similarly discovered in short-term volunteers an opportunity to accomplish vital overseas work while educating about the needs. Volunteers commit to time periods from one week to one year in which they offer service overseas. Once back in the States, many of these short-term volunteers become active supporters of more traditional overseas work.

One parish developed its own version of job sharing when a retired executive refused to act as board chair because of an anticipated extended stay in the South during winter months. A very busy professional agreed to assume the role during those months if his counterpart carried the load the other nine months.

Each religious education community will want to consider possible applications to the short-term volunteer concept. Such applications will prove more productive when they consider several characteristics of the short-term volunteer. Steve McCurly and Rick Lynch suggest these characteristics:

1. More general interests
2. Recruited by various techniques
3. Seeking definition
4. Motivated by recognition of personal achievement

The first characteristic, more general interests, points to the notion that short-term volunteers have a more general or superficial allegiance to an organization or cause. The short-term volunteer may agree to help plan one youth fellowship activity but does not have a deep commitment to long-term youth ministry.

McCurly and Lynch point out that short-termers respond to the task, not the cause, as they accept responsibility. For example, the short-term volunteer may accept responsibility for the craft table of the Vacation Bible School because of personal interest and skill in crafts, as opposed to the more traditional volunteer who did whatever was necessary to accomplish the V.B.S. Presumably, the latter was motivated through underlying convictions about the relative benefit of children's work.

McCurly and Lynch note that short-term volunteers may best be considered specialists who need specific definition about duration and task. Whereas the traditional volunteer accepted a position of church treasurer recognizing the task as involving the fiscal life of the church in general, the short-term volunteers may require specifics of what is involved in heading the annual stewardship drive.

A relatively new concept, the volunteer agreement, aids in accomplishing the need for definition and duration (see chapter eleven on agreements in general). Nancy Macduff suggests that the agreement provides further benefit by elevating the self-esteem of volunteers through an acknowledgment that the task and the volunteer are very important. A sample of such an agreement appears on the next page.

Finally, McCurly and Lynch note that for short-term volunteers, moti-

SHORT-TERM VOLUNTEER AGREEMENT

Agreement made between _____ , short-term volunteer, and the Religious Education Department of Trinity Church, Anytown, U.S.A.

Task to be Accomplished:

_____

_____

_____

_____

Resources to be Provided by the Church:

_____

_____

_____

_____

Resources to be Provided by the Volunteer:

_____

_____

_____

_____

Duration of Agreement:

Begin Date: _____   End Date: _____

Volunteer: _____ Date: _____

Director of R.E.: _____ Date: _____

This agreement is made with the understanding that both the volunteer and the church are under no legally binding obligation.

vation stems from recognition of personal accomplishment. While most traditional volunteers find satisfaction in the knowledge that the best teachers are chosen as department directors, short-term volunteers do not intend to commit to such time-bound goals. Instead, a quarterly appreciation banquet or an announcement in the local newspaper stimulates them to teach an elective for the quarter.

These characteristics point to several opportunities for response which arise from the move toward short-term volunteers. A brief exploration of these seems necessary.

Opportunities for Response

The move toward short-term volunteerism may make it necessary to restructure some of the jobs within the religious education department. A department's secretary, for example, may give way to a Monday afternoon typist, while another volunteer assumes the responsibility of other secretarial duties.

Further, once these tasks have been designated, the likelihood of rapid turnover in the volunteer program makes the development of job descriptions even more compelling. One short-term religious education volunteer resigned early and refused to reenlist simply because staff members did not agree on her role and act upon that agreement.

Also, short-term religious education volunteerism will necessitate a more time-consuming and costly training program. Frequent turnover obviously means more untrained assistance to follow. It may be appropriate to look to more long-term volunteers as trainers of those who perform the actual religious education functions in the short run.

On a more positive note, the move toward short-term volunteers implies the infusion of fresh ideas into the organization on a regular basis. Historically, John Wesley insisted that his preachers move from one location to another frequently so as to provide exposure to new gifts and graces for both the church and the preacher. A similar phenomenon exists among several modern faith groups. Like modern itinerants, the short-term religious education volunteer brings new perspective to the task. Of course, to gain maximum benefit from this turnover, it becomes absolutely necessary for a long-term volunteer or paid professional to utilize the concept of the exit interview (see chapter twenty-four).

The relationship between long- and short-term volunteers may become crucial in the development of the overall program. While conceivably long-term volunteers may look down on their short-term counterparts as less committed and even less vital to the organization, the converse may well develop. Professional staff, recognizing and communicating the importance of both long- and short-term volunteers, should create a climate of interdependency. In fact, long-term volunteers do provide a necessary element of stability to the overall ministry. Also, short-term volunteers often provide the bursts of enthusiasm necessary to accomplish a task.

While some of these opportunities will undoubtedly enhance the overall quality of the religious education program, others, without careful adjustment, may threaten that quality. At any rate, the successful program will want to adapt to the concept of short-term volunteers, even if leaders feel long-term volunteers would be preferable.

For Further Reading

Barna, George. *The Frog in the Kettle*. Ventura, Calif.: Regal, 1990.

Lasch, Christopher. *The Culture of Narcissism*. New York: Warner, 1989.

Macduff, Nancy. *Volunteer Recruiting And Retention*. Walla Walla, Wash.: Macduff/Bunt, 1985.

McCurly, Steve and Rick Lynch. *Essential Volunteer Management*. Downers Grove, Ill.: V.M. Systems/Heritage Arts, 1989.

Naisbitt, John and Patricia Aburdene. *Re-inventing the Corporation*. New York: Warner, 1985.

Ringer, Robert. *Looking Out for Number One*. New York: Fawcett, 1991.

Chapter Seventeen

Keeping and Motivating Volunteers

Former President Harry Truman is quoted as saying, "Leaders are people who can get others to do what they don't want to do—and make them like doing it." Perhaps nowhere in the realm of leadership are there such tremendous obstacles to motivating others than when the task involves motivating volunteers. Conversely, however, nowhere do such powerful resources for motivation exist as those in the religious community. In this chapter, we shall explore briefly several popular motivation theories and conclude by advancing a concept of motivation unique to the religious community.

Needs Theories

Everyone has needs. In fact, each of us harbors his or her own individual set of needs. Several motivation theories build upon the categorization of these needs.

For instance, Abraham Maslow in his book, *Motivation and Personality*, describes motivation in terms of a pyramid of needs. These can be summarized:

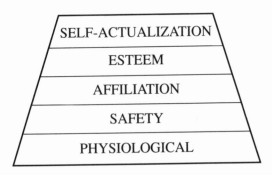

SELF-ACTUALIZATION
ESTEEM
AFFILIATION
SAFETY
PHYSIOLOGICAL

The pyramid moves from basic needs of immediate survival such as the need for air or food (physiological needs) all the way to the need to achieve or find fulfillment in accomplishment (self-actualization needs).

Simply put, Maslow contends that motivation occurs at the level of current need. For example, one will find little success recruiting any religious education volunteer by offering monetary compensation (approaching physiological needs) when the current need of the recruit's life involves a sense of belonging within the local church (affiliation needs).

Vance Packard in his book, *The Hidden Persuaders*, noted that advertisers target their product appeals to eight hidden needs. Unlike Maslow, Packard does not suggest a hierarchical arrangement for the eight, which include the need for:

1. Security
2. Reassurance of self-worth
3. Ego gratification
4. Being creative
5. Loving and being loved
6. Power
7. Roots
8. Immortality

Several of these needs could also apply to the persuasion of volunteers. Many persons accept positions as CCD or Sunday school paraprofessionals, for example, in response to the satisfaction the job brings. One such volunteer commented, "It's something I know I can do."

Other persons may volunteer for the same task from a need to bring creative expression to the biblical message or their own personal faith. "I just want a way to tell others what Jesus means to me," explained an evangelical volunteer.

The successful motivator of volunteers will need to recognize that not every potential volunteer has the same need. Further, each volunteer requires ongoing motivational fulfillment in the meeting of his or her unique needs.

Similar to the approaches of Maslow and Packard, W.C. Schultz identified three needs which human beings satisfy only through interpersonal relationships. These include the need to:

1. Exert control
2. Show affection
3. Find inclusion

Schultz's Interpersonal Needs Theory suggests that people are motivated to fulfill these three needs. Obviously each of the three could explain the motivation of religious education volunteers. Volunteers will find most rewarding those tasks which maximize opportunities to meet these three needs. Providing quality opportunities which meet these needs in volunteers will encourage them to respond by giving their best efforts to the organization.

Goal Theories

A more positive approach to the concept of motivation falls under the classification of goal theories. These theories build upon the notion that inner drives compel people to certain behaviors when they believe a personal goal is best met by performance.

The secret to motivation according to two popular theories in this classification, Expectancy Theory and Path-Goal Theory, lies in integrating organizational goals with the personal goals of the individual. A volunteer whose personal drive involves communicating religious faith to children will probably not find high motivation in teaching an adult Bible study. According to goal theories, the motivator will need to identify the volunteer's personal objectives and then correlate those with the task needs of the organization. Obviously, not all volunteers will find tasks which directly relate to their personal needs. Effective leadership will isolate that responsibility, however, which most clearly meets the volunteer participant's personal needs.

Consistency Theories

Yet another class of motivation theories rests upon the assumption that people do not like inconsistency in their lives. As a result, they will gravitate toward those experiences which ensure consistency. In religious education volunteers, for example, an inconsistency between the personal theological position and that espoused by the organization may decrease the tendency to volunteer for teaching a catechism class.

Consistency theories originated with the research team of Fritz Heider and Theodore Newcomb who suggested that a persuader, in order to be successful, will want to find a position of agreement (balance) with the person to be persuaded. If the receiver finds favor with the source, he/she will more likely find favor with the positions of the source in order to maintain internal balance.

Charles Osgood and Percy Tannenbaum brought consistency theories closer to the realm of volunteerism with the introduction of congruency theory. This theory does not necessarily involve two persons but may substitute two sets of information or positions observed by one person.

A volunteer who signs on to aid in an organization's fund-raising may discover questionable ethical practices used to motivate giving. While that volunteer supports the ministry of the organization, the inconsistency in fund-raising may well undermine the willingness to volunteer.

The prolife organization, Operation Rescue, provides an interesting case study. The reason many potential volunteers fail to align with that group can best be described in terms of consistency theories. On the one hand, these interested individuals strongly hold the right to life position. They supported their position by volunteering with other prolife organizations in the past. These same people cannot volunteer with Operation Rescue, however, because of internal inconsistencies created by the group's civil disobedience tactics. In short, only those who hold prolife positions, and who believe that in certain circumstances illegal protest is acceptable, find consistency within the ranks of Operation Rescue's volunteers.

Power/Authority Approaches

A thread which weaves through several of these motivation theories concerns the issues of power and authority. Power, as used here is not manipulative power of one person over another, but rather the responsibility one has within a position and the authority that goes with that position. One might question, "Where do I as a leader secure the power (authority) necessary to influence others to volunteer?" The answer, say French and Raven, usually involves sources of authority. These include reward, coercive, legitimate, expert, and charismatic power.

Reward power stems from the control that leadership has over those rewards which others receive. Secular businesses and industry capitalize on reward power to a great extent. An employee motivated to perform certain tasks in exchange for a paycheck at the end of the month has been motivated by reward power.

Religious education rewards often appear in less tangible forms than a paycheck. Those who volunteer to stay on a Christian education committee for the upcoming quarter because last quarter's planning retreat offered such warm fellowship have been motivated through reward power. One church invited all religious education volunteers to an annual appreciation banquet. The excellent meal and quality entertainment provided adequate reward to keep people volunteering.

Coercive power operates on the basis of controlling punishments, rather than rewards. In the business world, some may find motivation to perform through supervisors who have the authority to fire, for example.

While most religious organizations hesitate to fire volunteers (see chapter eighteen), other forms of coercive power do sometimes emerge. One man reported that he felt he must volunteer for the visitation program of his local church since the pastor viewed those who did not volunteer as "less spiritual." Often, coercive power appears in subtle, even unconscious ways in the motivation of religious volunteers.

The phrase "legitimate power" ought not suggest that other forms of power are somehow illegitimate or less legitimate. The term stems from the legitimacy that comes from a position of authority which is accepted by others. A parent who insists, "Do it because I said so," may be appealing to the legitimate power of parental authority.

Churches which use a spiritual mentor with new members provide that person with the legitimate power necessary to recruit volunteers. Many religious organizations operate under an organizational structure denoted by strong central authority. Legitimate power is pivotal to the operation of such a system.

A word of caution concerning the ethical use of legitimate power seems appropriate. One religious education volunteer who refused to perform a certain task because of personal convictions was attacked by the organization's leadership with the challenge, "I can't believe you wouldn't submit to those in authority as the scripture commands." It seems imperative that leaders exercise extreme caution when utilizing legitimate power. It is never appropriate to usurp others' rights, or be self-serving with this form of power.

The phrase "expert power" concerns the power held by an individual with special knowledge or information in a particular area. Perhaps children intuitively sense expert power at work when they chant, "I know something you don't know."

An industrialist who held a Masters degree in Business Administration agreed to accept the volunteer position of chair of the church's Administrative Council on the condition that "we operate with sound business practice, not just be sloppy because we're the church." Simply put, he appealed to use his expert power in dealings with other volunteers on the committee. That church enjoyed a very successful year at least in part as a result of yielding to his criteria for volunteering.

Charismatic power refers to the power held by those individuals who possess personally attracting qualities. The biblical character David provides an excellent example. While it is true David had legitimate power as a result of being God's anointed, Saul feared most David's charismatic power. Those who danced in the streets comparing the two men's accomplishments focused attention on the differences in their interpersonal skills.

Using charismatic power to entice people to volunteer may work for those who possess such power. Those church leaders less effective interpersonally may want to rely on highly charismatic, respected volunteers to recruit others. An obvious drawback to the use of such power stems from the fact that an entire program may develop around the personality of just one person, and a mass exodus may occur if that person leaves.

Reward power, coercive power, legitimate power, expert power, and charismatic power establish the limits of resources available to most secular motivators. Those who seek to motivate and recruit religious education volunteers may effectively utilize these and the previously mentioned theoretical approaches. In addition, however, these managers have at their disposal a sixth source of power—the power of divine summons.

Divine summons, or the personal mandate of God to perform a particular task, provided the power which prompted volunteerism in a host of biblical accounts. Moses "volunteered" to stand before Pharaoh when God spoke from the burning bush. Amos, the shepherd, became a volunteer prophet at the prodding of the Lord. Paul's vision from God caused him to volunteer for missionary service in Macedonia. The inner urging that God would fight the battle prompted David to volunteer to stand before Goliath.

Perhaps the greatest biblical picture comes from the recruiter known as Nehemiah. Nehemiah sought to recruit volunteers to assist in the rebuilding of the walls of Jerusalem. His pool of potential recruits included only those people who for the past several years had lived on top of the rubble and been largely unmoved. In three days, Nehemiah accomplished more than what had been done in the previous thirteen years. In chapter 2, verse 12 of the book which bears his name, Nehemiah explains, "I had not told anyone what my God had put in my heart to do for Jerusalem." Later he explains his motivation principles with these words, "I told them about the gracious hand of my God upon me...they replied, 'let us start rebuilding.' So they began this good work" (verse 18, NIV).

What recruiters for the modern religious program would not give for such a quick and enthusiastic response! The people volunteered and then worked hard because they sensed God's. The call of God acted as a supra-ordinary legitimate power. It might be labeled the power of "divine summons."

Of course we would not suggest stirring up people to volunteer with a "God told me to tell you" approach. Nor does this imply that every volunteer must have a specific call to a specific position. Instead, why not encourage potential recruits to prayerfully consider where God would have them become involved in the religious education program of the church.

David McKenna in his book *Renewing Our Ministry* compares ministry to marriage. He writes, "In a lifetime of ministry or marriage, passions will rise and fall; dreams will move in and out of focus. More often than not, the time will come when only the external commitment—'till death do us part'—will hold ministry or marriage together." To which we only add, such motivation provides the heart and soul of both professional and volunteer ministry.

For Further Reading

French, R.P., and B. Raven. "The Basis of Social Power." In *Group Dynamics*, ed. D. Cartright and A. Zonder, New York: Harper & Row, 1960.

Heider, Fritz. *The Psychology of Interpersonal Relations*. New York: Wiley, 1958.

Maslow, Abraham H. *Motivation and Personality*. New York: Harper & Row, 1954.

McKenna, David. *Renewing Our Ministry*. Waco, Tex.: Word, 1986.

Newcomb, Theodore. "An Approach to the Study of Communicative Acts." *Psychological Review* 60 (1953), pp. 393-404.

Osgood, Charles, and Percy Tannenbaum. "The Principle of Congruity in the Prediction of Attitude Change." *Psychological Review* 62 (1955), pp. 42-55.

Packard, Vance. *The Hidden Persuaders*. New York: Pocket Books, 1964.

Schultz, W.C. *FIRO: A Three Dimensional Theory of Interpersonal Behavior*. New York: Holt, Rinehart and Winston, 1958.

Chapter Eighteen

Encouraging Some
Volunteers to Leave

To dwell above with saints we love,
Oh won't that be glory.
But to dwell below with saints we know,
Now there's a different story.

It would certainly come as no shock to the unknown author of this brief poem that sometimes conflict erupts in the church. Tragically, that conflict can often involve religious education volunteers.

The youth leaders of a small church in the Midwest served in a volunteer religious education capacity. With enthusiasm they planned activities for the teens, supervised those activities, and offered spiritual direction for the junior and senior high set. While the husband and wife team prepared well and took their responsibilities seriously, they did not relate well with the teens. Attendance at the Sunday evening youth meeting declined dramatically. Parents began to insist that the Board of Deacons impose a change in leadership. But, how does one fire willing volunteers?

The same question plagued the home church of Mrs. Smith (not her real name). She acted as the religious education treasurer of the church, a volunteer position she had held for more than twenty years. Mrs. Smith had served the church well through some very difficult times. Older members recalled the days when the income of the church, being too low to meet expenses was greatly supplemented from Mrs. Smith's personal funds. Today, however, the church's growth pattern meant lots of new young families and plenty of resources. Yet, Mrs. Smith avoided progressive thinking in fiscal matters. On one occasion she had even refused to pay a bill approved by the board, saying when they failed to behave responsibly she would still maintain good stewardship standards. Congregation members believed Mrs. Smith had to be replaced, yet hesitated to hurt her after so many years of voluntary service.

Clearly, even in voluntary religious programs, conflict plays a prominent role. Someone has gone so far as to suggest the inevitability of conflict. Perhaps Murphy's Law, "If anything can go wrong, it will go wrong," ought to carry a corollary, "If there can be conflict; there will be conflict." In spite of obvious problems with a volunteer, a local church pastor admitted, "If no one's complaining, I'm not doing anything."

Where does conflict come from? Perhaps if we isolate the sources, we will be better able to minimize conflict. Experts agree that primarily conflict arises from three sources. These include:

1. Differences in input
2. Fixed availability of resources
3. Interpersonal rivalries

Differences in Input

Much conflict can be traced to differences in input received by the persons involved in the dispute. Information differences, for example, often lead to conflict. If the youth leaders mentioned earlier in this chapter assumed their role involved planning for the youth, while the youth intended to make their own plans, conflict inevitably looms. These differing assumptions probably came from different experiences ("input").

Similarly, interest differences lead to conflict. A volunteer whose primary interest in Vacation Bible School lies in evangelizing unchurched youngsters is on a collision course with those whose interest lies in teaching biblical truth to youngsters from the church family.

Differences in beliefs or values may also stimulate conflict. Many theological conflicts in local churches arise because one group holds a value or belief in contradiction to others in the group.

Recognizing that differences in input often lead to conflict can aid the manager of volunteers in avoiding such conflict. Information must be clearly communicated to everyone involved. Interests must be announced in advance and matched to available volunteer positions. Ideas about values and beliefs must be exchanged and examined. Often religious toleration develops (Rom 14:5), but where that is an impossibility, early addressing of issues leads to early averting of conflict.

One approach which forestalls conflict involves the use of a job description for all volunteer positions (see chapter seven). The properly worded description indicates those areas for which a volunteer will accept responsibility. It may also include areas outside the scope of the task and should note the duration of the assignment. For example, had Mrs. Smith, the treasurer mentioned earlier, been working under the authority of a job description, she might have anticipated a one-year term, wherein deciding which bills warranted payment fell outside the scope of her authority. Further, if she failed to live up to the standards in the description, the conflict might well be directed toward an object (performance of the job description), rather than people (Mrs. Smith and members of the board).

While many churches see job descriptions as too formal and confining to volunteers, the opposite may in reality prove true. Recognizing job descriptions as declarations of the boundaries of a task often provides greater freedom to function within those boundaries. Recognizing this truth, many volunteers actually insist on a job description before agreeing to volunteer.

Fixed Availability of Resources

In addition to differences in input, the fixed availability of certain valued resources often leads to conflict. It requires imagination to see this source of conflict at work on a worldwide scale. Limits of commodities such as foodstuffs, money, or oil can ultimately lead to such global conflicts.

In the religious education program, however, more subtle resources such as space, position, time, or authority may be involved. Anywhere a resource of value exists in fixed quantities, the potential for conflict exists. When those resources fall into short supply, that potential becomes even greater.

One church made its fellowship hall available to the local Girl Scout troop on the first Tuesday of each month. The arrangement worked well until an adult visitation training class attempted to schedule a special meeting on the first Tuesday. Conflict erupted over whose interests took precedence. At root the limited number of fellowship halls (one) led to the altercation.

In another setting, the dispute arose over whether the senior citizens group or the education committee had the right to expect the pastor to attend their simultaneous meetings on a particular evening. The fixed resource, pastor's time, became the actual source of the conflict.

While in a few situations it may prove feasible to expand the resource pool by buying more supplies or allocating more hours, conflicts of this nature usually require give-and-take compromise. Once again, communication provides the key. A sign-up sheet for rooms in high demand, or an earlier invitation to the pastor may create a better utilization scenario. In other cases, participants demonstrate an ongoing unwillingness or inability to compromise. In those cases, a third source of conflict may be at the root.

Interpersonal Rivalries

John's released time class had tried several different curriculum alternatives and a wide variety of teaching techniques when John observed, "Some of the people in the class wouldn't like the teacher if he were Jesus Christ himself." John's comment points to the third source of conflict, interpersonal rivalries.

Simply put, some personalities just do not match. Even with equal information banks and unlimited resource pools, certain volunteers will live in the midst of conflict.

A small church pastor identified one such person recently. He noted, "She always speaks 'for a lot of us who feel this way.' The others," he continued, "don't ever seem involved in the unrest, however."

It behooves the leader of volunteers to carefully analyze the "whys" of such situations in an attempt to uncover any underlying needs. Some volunteers may crave the attention conflict brings. Others may hold buried personal or psychological needs which provide opportunities for effective ministry. Many times persons have simply volunteered for tasks for which they are not suited. They might belong at some other level on the religious education lattice.

Leadership could minimize interpersonal rivalries by having an improved knowledge of potential volunteers before acceptance. Often churches view volunteers as such a scarce commodity that those who emerge become quickly enlisted. Those organizations which use an application/evaluation process (see chapter ten) often find the pool of potential volunteers increases since the holding of a position becomes a matter of prestige within the organization.

Of course, recognizing these sources of conflict will not eliminate their impact. Nor will implementing our suggestions for dealing with each source eradicate the problem entirely. In short, conflict will exist in every organization, including those staffed by religious education volunteers. Only two courses of action remain when conflict does arise — continued conflict or resolution of the conflict. The flow chart on the next page highlights the two, along with the procedures and results of following each course of action.

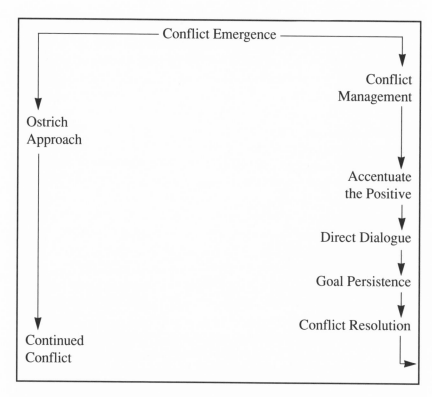

Many times religious organizations choose to deal with conflict by pretending it does not exist. Such "burying of the head in sand" may stem from a belief that conflict in the Christian community provides a bad witness. Embarrassment may also surface that we do not "operate in harmony," since we fail to see eye-to-eye on every point.

Regardless of the reasons, the Ostrich Approach seldom solves problems. Conflict cannot ultimately be ignored, it must be managed.

As the flow chart suggests, effective conflict management incorporates a three-step process.

1. Accentuate the positive
2. Direct dialogue
3. Goal persistence

From the eye of the storm, the search for positive aspects of conflict often seems futile. Several positives often emerge from conflict, however. For example, conflict may:

1. Point to deeper organizational problems
2. Encourage open discussion on broader issues
3. Force organizational oneness in finding solutions

4. Allow for creative expression in proposing alternatives

At any rate, the manager of conflict will want to focus on the strengths which the present debate can bring to both the organization and the individuals involved.

Often conflict causes people to discuss the issues with everyone *but* the religious education volunteer involved. Conversely, direct dialogue refers to meeting the issues head on with the person or persons embroiled. Such an approach becomes increasingly significant in light of biblical injunctions to deal with conflict issues first with those who have wronged us.

When the announcement came that one Director of Christian Education intended to take a new position, a lay volunteer with whom there had been several strong disagreements stopped in to say goodbye. "I just wanted you to know," he offered, "while I've not always agreed with you, I've always known right where you stood. I appreciate that." Direct, honest, open communication has no substitute in conflict resolution.

Even when all other avenues of conflict management have failed and dismissing a staff volunteer looms inevitable, direct dialogue gets the matter quickly resolved. In these cases, it is important for the supervisor of volunteers to have clearly documented the reasons for dismissal. Inasmuch as it is possible, the dismissal should be handled privately with the volunteer. Care should be taken that the dismissed volunteer does not leave the faith group as a result of the dismissed experience. In all likelihood he/she could serve very effectively at some other level of the religious educator lattice. The approach should be designed to maximize the possibility of both parties maintaining positive feelings about the organization and individuals. At any rate, circumstances should allow both individuals and the organization to get back to other matters.

Those matters in the case of the organization will involve program goals. The third step in effective conflict management, goal persistence, brings combatants back to the real issues at hand.

Commenting on the pro-football career of running back Walter Payton, a sportscaster noted, "In his career, Payton rushed for more than nine miles of total yardage." "Especially significant," quipped his colleague, "when you consider he got knocked down every 4.6 yards."

Often conflict becomes so time and attention consuming that it undermines the established goals of a ministry. It is tempting to reflect only on getting knocked down and forget to get up and persist toward the goal. As an ongoing process, and clearly at the point of conflict resolution, effective conflict managers refocus the efforts of all members of the team on the long-term purposes of the organization.

This three-step approach —accentuate the positive, direct dialogue, and goal persistence— does not promise a panacea. When conflict comes, it inevitably leads to some pain. Dismissing staff, perhaps most especially volunteer staff, is never easy. On the other hand, such effective conflict management maximizes the benefits of conflict and minimizes the hurts.

Termination of Volunteers Form

(Adapted from Kenneth Gangel)

	Accomplished	Unsure	Not Accomplished
Task was Understood	___	___	___
Evaluation was Completed	___	___	___
Volunteer Comprehended Evaluation	___	___	___
Task Cannot Be Changed	___	___	___
Other Volunteer Tasks Un-Available/Inappropriate	___	___	___
Notification Well in Advance of Termination	___	___	___
Final Interview Conducted	___	___	___
Spiritual/Personal Follow-up (if appropriate)	___	___	___

For Further Reading

Borisoff, Deborah, and David A. Victor. *Conflict Management: A Communication Skills Approach.* Englewood Cliffs, N.J.: Prentice-Hall, 1989.

Christie, Les. *Unsung Heroes.* Grand Rapids, Mich.: Zondervan, 1987. [Rereleased in 1992 as *How to Recruit and Train Volunteer Youth Workers.*]

Gangel, Kenneth. *Feeding and Leading.* Wheaton, Ill: Victor, 1989.

Macduff, Nancy. *Volunteer Recruiting and Retention.* Walla Walla, Wash.: Macduff/Bunt, 1985.

McCurley, Steve, and Rick Lynch. *Essential Volunteer Management.* Washington, D.C.: VMSystems, 1989.

McCurley, Steve, and Sue Vineyard. *101 Ideas for Volunteer Programs.* Downers Grove, Ill.: Heritage Arts, 1986.

Senter III, Mark. *Recruiting Volunteers in the Church*, 2d ed. Wheaton, Ill.: Victor, 1990.

Part VI

Administering Volunteer
Religious Education Programs

Chapter Nineteen

Administering the Program

A retired legal secretary with many years of experience in office practice agreed to work part-time in the office of a Christian organization. A few months later when asked about her volunteer work, she made this observation, "It seems as if it's always harder to work for Christians. Why are they such poor supervisors?"

While recognizing her statement as an overgeneralization, one must also acknowledge a dearth of effective administrative leadership in the church. Ironically, she used the term "supervisor" to describe her frustration. In fact supervision is a specialized term in education that refers to facilitating instructional improvement. We have explored that need in Part IV of this book. While professional religious educators may or may not be lacking in these supervisory skills, they do often demonstrate an additional lack of ability in administering the religious education program. The latter deficiency is addressed in this section. Several possible explanations for the administrative void exist.

Perceived Incompatibilities

A widespread view of administration as a secular (even "fleshly" or "worldly") endeavor antithetical to Christianity seems to prevail in the church. David McKenna, president of Asbury Theological Seminary, wrote an article entitled "Administration as Ministry" in Kenneth Kinghorn's *A Celebration Of Ministry*. In the chapter McKenna relates the account of a woman who viewed with despair his initial postseminary position as Dean of Men at a leading Christian college. He quotes her as lamenting, "Oh, and I prayed so hard you would go into the ministry." For this woman, and for countless other people, any form of administration was not ministry.

On the other hand, principles of administration contain nothing categorically contrary to Christian teaching. In fact, such a view seems to ignore the fact that "Administration" appears in the scriptural list of the gifts of the Spirit, thus indicating the possibility of a special empowerment for that ministry. Of course, unscrupulous administrators do exist whose lives fail to exemplify Christian principles. Those lives may well fall short of effective administrative principles as well.

Lack of Training

Many leaders of Christian organizations lack formal training in the area of administrative or organizational communication. Christian colleges, universities, and seminaries have seemed reluctant to add such training to curriculum.

One pastor five years out of seminary lamented that he saw administration as his greatest deficiency. While willing, he sensed a lack of necessary skills to administer the volunteer staff of his growing flock. The lack of printed materials from a Christian perspective provides yet another evidence of the inadequate training in administration for church leaders. With a few notable exceptions like Don Dayton and Ted Engstrom, few apparently feel qualified to write in the field from a theological perspective. This fact leads to a third explanation for the lack of skilled administrative personnel in the church.

Lack of Theology

Perhaps as a result of the previous two problems, no sound theology of administration exists. That which lacks theological underpinnings does not exist long in the religious community.

At the very least, such a theology should consider:
1. The role of the Holy Spirit in empowering administrators in the church.
2. The concept of servanthood and its compatibility with administration.
3. The role of prayer in the life of the administrator.
4. Issues of delegation of authority as they relate to administration in the church.

Other Perspectives of Administration

In the absence of a uniquely Christian view of administration, we must now turn our attention to some basic secular understandings, gleaning possible principles applicable to the administration of volunteers.

Douglas McGregor in *The Human Side Of Enterprise* noted two diametrically opposed theories of administration at work in the industrial world. He labeled these Theory X and Theory Y. (While he uses the term "management," we will use the term "administration" for greater applicability to religious education contexts.)

Theory X administration builds upon an understanding of human nature such that people:

1. Dislike work, and thus avoid it where possible
2. Must be coerced into performance
3. Prefer to be closely directed

One religious education director verbally expressed confidence and appreciation in the volunteers. In practice, however, he constantly checked up, overruled, and insisted on alternate approaches. This leader obviously held to a Theory X view of administration and directed people closely as a result of those beliefs. One might argue that the entire topic of volunteerism countermands these Theory X principles. Volunteers by definition have not avoided, and need not be coerced into performance.

Our attention quickly turns then to the foundational principles which support Theory Y administration. These include the notions that:

1. Work is natural
2. People often accept and seek responsibility
3. People want to creatively solve problems

Theory Y administration seems to more readily lend itself to the administration of volunteers. It provides a more scripturally accurate view of the nature of human beings. The view also lends itself to a more team-oriented approach to the functions of administration. Those who hold to the Theory Y perspectives see administration as a coordinating of the efforts of others rather than demanding performance from them.

Rensis Likert in the book, *New Patterns Of Management*, described four approaches to management (again, we will use the word "administration" rather than "management"). These build from McGregor's theories, with the first two encompassing Theory X philosophy and the latter two Theory Y.

1. Exploitative authoritative
2. Benevolent authoritative
3. Consultative
4. Participative

Tight control and authority characterizes the exploitative authoritative leadership style. Workers, whether volunteer or professional, are viewed as interchangeable parts in the overall process of meeting organizational goals. Administrators who use the exploitative authoritative style usually experience high rates of worker turnover. However, they do not recognize this as a problem, so long as others willingly take their place for at least a short time. Increasingly, research indicates a high degree of ineffectiveness in the exploitative authoritative style.

Benevolent authoritative administrators soften the autocratic style somewhat. Workers still have little, if any, voice in actual decisions, but comments and even complaints are allowed. The "open-door" policy of many corporations typifies the style, since the door stands ajar to worker input, which is usually ignored.

The consultative administrator style closely resembles benevolent authoritative with a slight shift toward Theory Y administration. In the consultative approach, the administrator consults with workers prior to decision making. The administrator still, however, makes unilateral decisions.

Participative organizational style encourages workers to participate fully in goal setting as well as day-to-day decision making. The team approach of Japanese industrial firms provides an example, as do more and more American corporations in the information age.

The chart below not only integrates Likert's and McGregor's approaches to administration, but emphasizes the effects of each administrative style as well.

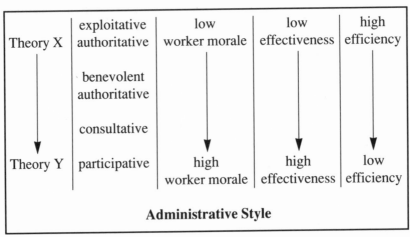

Theory X	exploitative authoritative	low worker morale	low effectiveness	high efficiency
	benevolent authoritative			
	consultative			
Theory Y	participative	high worker morale	high effectiveness	low efficiency

Administrative Style

The administrator of volunteers, as any administrator of human resources, must select the approach which best meets the needs and projected outcome of the current circumstances. No one style works in every circumstance.

For example, the administrator of a parachurch youth ministry reported that he used a highly participative approach with the volunteers who worked directly with programing and teens. Frequently the group overruled his opinions as to the best approach for solving a particular problem. He intuitively chose that style in order to create the most effective ministry possible.

The same administrator dealt with the volunteer who acted as secretary-receptionist in a much more directive style. Here, effectiveness posed less of a goal, since the most effective office procedures had long since been agreed upon. Instead, efficiency, getting the most done in the allotted time, provided the primary motivation.

Since volunteers come and go at will, and are provided little incentive to work other than the pride of accomplishment, the effective administrator will want to choose that style which allows for the greatest worker involvement and thus maximizes morale. For example, where doctrinal distinctives allow for several different curricula, Sunday school teachers should have a hand in selecting material.

Sometimes, however, the opinions and needs of the workers will not coincide with the need for task accomplishment. Here, the administrative style selection becomes more difficult.

Robert Blake and Jane Mouton in *The Managerial Grid* attempted to deal with the dilemma schematically (again, we will apply management principles to religious education administration). Recognizing that most administrative circumstances require concern for both people and the task at hand, they rated administrators from 1 to 9, low to high in each category. A particular administrative style for a given circumstance could thus be plotted on the grid.

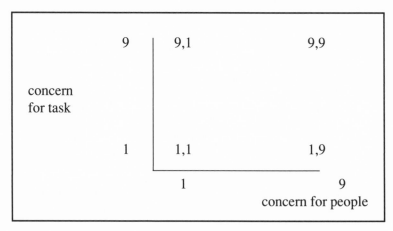

9,1 administrators exemplify a high efficiency in task accomplishment, without much regard for people. Conversely, a 1,9 administrator may spend so much time dealing with the concerns of people that there is little task accomplishment. Of course the ideal 9,9 administrator, high on task and high on people, seldom appears, but gratefully most religious education leadership proves better than 1,1. Ratings may show a leader whatever needs improvement.

Thus far we have explored selection of the correct leadership style for various circumstances, especially as it relates to the administration of volunteers. It remains to note what the administration actually "does" once the style for "doing" has been selected. That is, what are the functions, or purposes, of administration?

The literature states that the six functions of administration include:

1. Planning
2. Organizing
3. Staffing
4. Implementing
5. Controlling
6. Evaluating

While we have included separate sections on several of these areas, a brief overview seems in order.

Planning involves developing an overall purpose as well as the objectives and activities necessary to accomplish that purpose. An administrator engages in planning when discussing the mission priorities (see chapter six) of the Christian Education Department with the church board, as well as when determining teaching objectives or youth fellowship activities with the volunteer staff. At every level, planning builds the bridge from where the organization is now to where we would like for it to be at some point in the future.

Organizing sometimes is considered an advanced stage of planning in that it involves determining the time line and task requirements to make plans happen. Organizational plans should include sufficient detail to allow each member of the team to begin task accomplishment. Also, the completion date should clearly appear on plan sheets to allow a space for the administrator of the project to return and follow up on plans.

Staffing includes the processes necessary to fill positions in the organization. The administrator will discover specific staffing responsibilities relating to individual projects as well as the ongoing challenge of keeping filled the regular roles required by the organization. Elsewhere in this volume (chapters eight to fifteen) we have considered in detail the staffing process of selecting, recruiting, and training volunteers.

Implementing involves actually putting into action those plans created in the planning phase and developed in the organizing and staffing phases. It could be argued that implementation becomes more critical in the volunteer religious education organization than among paid staff since there exists a greater likelihood that volunteers will ignore or forget plans and fail to carry them out. On the other hand, experience suggests that where personnel, paid or volunteer, have adequate input in the planning process they will want to implement without much direction.

Controlling is very similar to the implementation phase of administration but with some unique characteristics. The greatest difference between the two functions lies in timing. Whereas implementing puts the plans in motion initially, controlling measures and corrects ongoing performance against initial objectives. Controlling depends upon an adequate understanding of the mission, objectives, and up-to-date information about current progress. One administrator of volunteers was appalled to hear the first monthly report from the volunteer treasurer, "Well, the money came in, and the money went out." Wisely, that administrator insisted on more conventional bookkeeping and reporting in order to better perform the control function.

Evaluating, an often overlooked phase of administration, we discuss in chapters fourteen and twenty-four. The importance, however, of properly evaluating both volunteers and programs cannot be overemphasized. For too long the religious community has engaged in evaluation only under the rubric, "We've always done it that way." The effective administrator of volunteers will question, "Why have we done it that way? Is that way still effective? Are there better ways?"

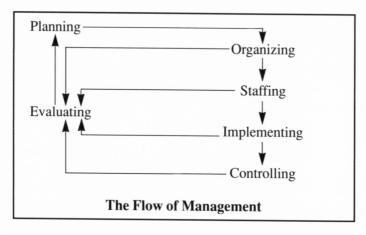

The Flow of Management

In summary, whatever style of leadership the administrator of volunteers chooses, the functions of planning, organizing, staffing, implementing, controlling, and evaluating must be accomplished. The flow chart demonstrates each of the six, while emphasizing the particular importance of planning and evaluating in the ongoing process.

As the flow chart indicates, evaluating followed by a return to planning maximizes effectiveness at every stage in the administration process.

While the volunteer secretary's observation that religious programs are poorly administered may be true, it is not necessarily so. Utilizing just a few techniques of sound administrative principles can make the difference between a mediocre and an outstanding volunteer program.

For Further Reading

Blake, Robert, and Jane S. Mouton. *The Managerial Grid*. Houston: Gulf, 1964.

Dayton, Don, and Ted Engstrom. *Strategy for Leadership*. Old Tappan, N.J.: Revell, 1988.

Kinghorn, Kenneth Cain, ed. *A Celebration Of Ministry*. Wilmore, Ky.: Francis Asbury, 1982.

Likert, Rensis. *New Patterns of Management*. New York: McGraw-Hill, 1960.

McGregor, Douglas. *The Human Side Of Enterprise*. New York: McGraw-Hill, 1960.

Chapter Twenty

Climate and Context of the Volunteer Program

The name Spencer Silver is not exactly a household word. People rarely seek Spencer's autograph, and little children do not sing jingles about him. Yet anyone who has ever appreciated a little yellow "Post-it" note owes a debt of gratitude to Spencer Silver and to his employer, the 3-M corporation.

It began in the mid-1960s when Spencer, a research chemist, invented a glue that did not stick. At least it failed to bond permanently, but it would retain its tacky nature through several applications. Not surprisingly, marketers and executives at 3-M failed to see the benefit of such a product and decided scratch paper coated with the adhesive would not likely revolutionize their industry.

What is surprising, however, is that a decade and a half later, Spencer and a few colleagues who believed in his product remained on the 3-M payroll when the product did change the nature of office note-taking through Post-it notes.

In fact, during those many years several administrators rejected Spencer's project, but none rejected Spencer. No one said, "Quit fooling around and get back to work." By constrast, a conscious effort exists at 3-M to encourage employees to be creative and pursue their own product interests, however ridiculous those ideas might appear. The tremendous ultimate success of "Post-it" points to the wisdom of such a philosophy.

What 3-M provided for Spencer Silver, researchers often label "positive organizational climate." Organizational climate cannot be developed by a series of rules and regulations. It does not exist in training programs, evaluation techniques, or administrative styles in spite of the importance of these. Organizational climate is a composite of factors

177

that determine the atmosphere of the organization and thus provide degrees of encouragement to employees (or volunteers). Spencer Silver found an environment at 3-M that encouraged him to do the very best he could for the company.

Similarly, religious education programs operate in a unique organizational climate. This climate determines how volunteers perform, as well as how they account for the performance of others.

Mary had received all the materials necessary to begin the children's religious education ministry for her church. In addition, she had board approval to begin the project. Mary seemed to possess the skills necessary to accomplish this important ministry. Yet, nothing happened. Mary appeared too timid to take the action necessary to get the project rolling.

While initially Mary's pastor and other church leaders were perplexed, the answer may well lie in the concept of organizational climate. The real source of Mary's procrastination may emerge in the answers to questions like:

1. In what tangible ways have we demonstrated our confidence in Mary?

2. How have we communicated the importance of the task?

3. Based on past programs in this church, what can Mary expect to happen if she fails? If she succeeds?

4. Do we expect Mary's success?

Climate Dimensions

Like physical climate, organizational climate defies definition. Factors such as temperature, rainfall, atmospheric pressure, and humidity averaged over several years are considered physical climate. Similarly, such elements as volunteer attitudes toward one another, administrator expectations, problem-solving techniques, and the degree of appreciativeness averaged over time produce organizational climate.

George Litwin and Robert Stringer identify nine dimensions of organizational climate, each of which bears application to the religious education volunteer program. First, they suggest that *structure* helps mold the climate. Is the structural atmosphere loose and informal, or are proper channels emphasized? Do volunteers feel constrained by regulations or freed by the communication of appropriate procedures?

Responsibility, according to Litwin and Stringer comprises the second dimension of climate. The entrepreneurial spirit which trusts volunteers to accomplish a particular task and make decisions relating to that task relates to this dimension. This does not suggest that boundless autonomy yields the best organizational climate, but that volunteers do function best in a context of responsibility.

The third dimension, *reward*, relates to volunteers at the point of public appreciation. Are verbal rewards for performance frequent and genuine?

Risk, according to Litwin and Stringer, in appropriate doses provides therapy for the organizational climate. Volunteers need the privilege of taking chances on new approaches including, when necessary, the freedom to fail.

The relationships between volunteers may be characterized by both dimensions five and six. These the researchers label *warmth* and *support*. The degree of fellowship between and among volunteers and with the paid staff constitutes warmth, while support involves the help afforded in accomplishing the task.

Standards, which may include the importance of doing quality work as well as the ethical implications of task accomplishment, encapsulates the seventh dimension of Litwin and Stringer. Volunteers tend to perform at the level of perceived expectation; no higher, no lower.

The term *conflict* characterizes the eighth dimension of organizational climate. Often, satisfaction hinges upon administrators and co-volunteers tolerating differing opinions and honestly striving to identify and solve problems.

Litwin and Stringer use the term *identity* to describe the ninth and final dimension of organizational climate. Other authors have used "team spirit" to describe this dimension: feeling like he or she belongs to the total group process.

It should be noted that each of these nine dimensions constitutes a continuum leading to a more or less positive organizational climate. The administrator of volunteers could evaluate the climate of a particular volunteer program by objectively identifying the organization in each area. A more serious evaluation might be developed by adding a Likert-type scale and asking volunteers to anonymously provide the ratings. A sample of such a rating sheet appears on the next page.

Climate Types

Andrew Halpin and Donald Croft, in a study of organizational climate in schools, identified six climates which relate well to volunteer programs.

An *open* climate allows for a high degree of volunteer involvement in the decision-making process. Volunteers functioning in such a climate will

Volunteer Climate Profile

To assist in providing the best possible environment in which to volunteer, please rate our religious education program in the nine areas noted below. Circle one number for each dimension. Be as honest as possible. You need not add your name.

Dimension I Structure

informal				formal
1	2	3	4	5

Dimension II Responsibility

trusting				doubting
1	2	3	4	5

Dimension III Reward

appreciative				nonappreciation
1	2	3	4	5

Dimension IV Risk

innovative				unchanging
1	2	3	4	5

Dimension V Warmth

friendly				unfriendly
1	2	3	4	5

Dimension VI Support

supportive				nonsupportive
1	2	3	4	5

Dimension VII Standards

excellence				mediocre
1	2	3	4	5

Dimension VIII Conflict

open				closed
1	2	3	4	5

Dimension IX Identity

team effort				individual effort
1	2	3	4	5

demonstrate high morale and organizational loyalty.

In the *autonomous* climate, the administrator of volunteers may remain distanced from the staff. The group works well together, but support or warmth from leadership appears only rarely.

A *controlled* climate places a higher standard upon efficiency than on effectiveness. Volunteers roles begin and end with the meeting of institutional goals. Personal needs of volunteers are secondary.

The *familiar* climate in contrast to the controlled climate stresses volunteer relationships at the expense of efficiency. In decision making, effectiveness rises because the input of each volunteer is cherished.

An overbearing leader often leads to high conflict among the volunteers and low morale. Such conditions characterize the *paternalistic* climate. Such a style produces neither efficiency nor effectiveness in the organization's decision making since the only assistance afforded volunteers comes in the form of directives.

Finally, the *closed* climate appears similar to the paternalistic, except that even direction is absent. Volunteers are expected to perform without any input from administrators. Morale is low; turnover is high; efficiency and effectiveness are low.

Improving The Climate

Of course, the administrator of the religious education program will want to create the kind of open climate which fosters high volunteer motivation and morale and which makes the overall program as efficient and effective as possible. Several keys will, over time, help develop such a climate.

Key #1 Encourage Volunteer Input. For various reasons, many administrators seem unwilling to allow volunteers input regarding the best way to accomplish the task. Such an attitude fosters a sense of alienation and distrust rather than the warm team spirit indicative of an open climate.

Following the more formal business meeting, one administrator went around the room and asked each meeting participant what else they would like to say. Far from feeling put on the spot, volunteers reported a sense that leadership really valued their opinions.

Encouraging volunteer input necessitates, however, that the leadership of the program develop their own skills in listening. Even when encouraged, volunteers will not provide input for long if they sense their input is only a rote exercise and never acted upon. Empathetic listening is a must!

Key #2 Provide Positive Affirmation. Every human being harbors a need for appreciation. Unfortunately, the religious community often assumes that ministering to that need encourages unwholesome pride. Instead, frequent sincere public appreciation encourages volunteers to perform even more effectively.

A Sunday school teacher recently reported that he became a regular volunteer teacher when students expressed honest appreciation for his efforts as a substitute on a particular Sunday. He confessed that prior to that experience he had not seen himself as particularly capable of being a teacher. Conversely, he quipped, "I'm not in the choir anymore because people seemed more appreciative of my noninvolvement in that area."

Key #3 Disclose Information. Administrators utilize approaches to handling organizational information. Some operate from the position, "Tell them only what they need to know." By contrast, others conclude, "Tell them everything. It won't hurt them or the organization to know." The latter approach helps build a climate of openness in the volunteer organization.

Since information represents power, often volunteers view the withholding of information as a threat. Conversely, to share information includes sharing the power that information affords.

Further, information carries with it the implication that volunteers can be trusted. Such an atmosphere of open trust also motivates renewed excellence.

Key #4 Foster Enthusiasm. No one wants to remain trapped in a dead-end job. Similarly, volunteers yearn for a position of excitement; a place to really make a difference. Whatever honestly communicates the importance of each volunteer enhances the overall organizational climate. The administrator of volunteers will want to hold before the team the total mission of the program and each volunteer's role in accomplishing that mission.

Key #5 Build a Team Spirit. It is an established fact of organizational development that people support what they help determine. Whenever, therefore, the administrator of volunteers can offer decision-making authority to an individual, the entire group benefits. Some religious education programs have fostered the team spirit through such incentives as contests between departments, volunteer-of-the-month programs, "Meet the Volunteer" columns in church newsletters, or convincing a local newspaper to feature particular volunteers from time to time. Others use a meeting or a collective group for cook-outs, camp-outs, and other social functions.

While the product of the religious education department differs significantly from that of 3-M, the organizational climates ought to be very similar. In both cases, workers can find the environment stimulating and motivating. Administrators in either organization must consciously select the appropriate environment and put in place those plans which develop it.

For Further Reading

Halpin, Andrew W., and Donald B. Croft. *Organizational Climate of Schools*. Chicago: Midwest Administration Center, University of Chicago, 1963.

Ilsley, Paul J., and John A. Niemi. *Recruiting and Training Volunteers*. New York: McGraw-Hill, 1981.

Litwin, George H., and Robert A. Stringer Jr. *Motivation and Organizational Climate*. Cambridge: Harvard University Press, 1968.

Nayak, P. Ranganath, and John Ketteringham. "3-M's Little Yellow Note Pads." *Breakthroughs*. York: Arthur D. Little, 1986.

Chapter Twenty-One

Holding Effective Meetings
with Volunteers

When division threatened the volunteer program at Trinity Church, the leadership knew exactly what to do. They called a meeting. Everyone understood in advance the reason for the meeting. Discussion quickly produced a solution; the majority agreed on a course of action. A more effective volunteer program resulted.

While many modern religious education meetings do not have such happy endings, the account described above parallels a volunteer meeting recorded in Acts 6. A factional dispute in the ancient church arose among the volunteers because some saw the food distribution program as less than effective. The Twelve called a meeting to deal with the problem. Included on the agenda was a proposed solution calling for the creation of a new class of volunteers to focus on the performance of physical ministry. This, proponents reasoned, would allow more time for current volunteers (the Twelve) to perform religious education ministry and also would yield a more effective total program. The motion carried, and election of the new volunteers by consensus followed. The entire attitude with which everyone went back to work points to the meeting's success. The fact that others, drawn by the spirit of unity, soon joined the faithful further marks the successfulness of this key meeting.

Several significant factors insured the success of this meeting. An examination of each will help strengthen the modern volunteer meeting as well.

A Reason to Meet

As the members of the Jerusalem Christian religious community came together, no doubt existed in anyone's mind as to the purpose of the meeting. A particular problem prompted the gathering.

No one would argue that problems constitute the only valid reason for volunteers to meet. On the other hand, often the reason for holding a meeting could be summarized, "We meet tonight because it is the second Tuesday of the month." Perhaps a key reason for poor attendance and lack of enthusiasm rests in failure to issue a purpose.

One important means to communicate a meeting's purpose involves the printed agenda. A printed agenda distributed several days in advance gives participants an opportunity to formulate positions and prayerfully study issues. The agenda need not confine the discussion, only guide it. This sample agenda from the Religious Education Board of a small membership church in the Midwest demonstrates what we mean:

"You shall see greater things than these." John 1:50

Trinity Church
Religious Education Board Meeting
3/14/1993
7:00 pm

A. Devotions

B. Minutes 2/10/93

C. Treasurer's Report

	General Fund	Curriculum Fund	Memorial Fund
1. Balance 1/31/93	$3942.40	$70.00	$140.95
2. Balance 2/28/93	_____	_____	_____
3. Reconciliation with the budget			

D. Old Business

    1. Copier Maintenance

    2. Other Issues

E. New Business

    1. Religious Education Director's Report

    2. Reports of Standing Committees

    3. Plans for youth missions trip

    4. Plan for Vacation Bible School

    5. Other

Another church, anxious to avoid the traditional "old business," found new terminology brought a measure of creativity to their printed agenda.

RELIGIOUS EDUCATION COUNCIL

Trinity Church

November 18, 1993

7:15 p.m.

Proposed Agenda

Call To Order 7:15

Establishing Agenda

I. Celebrating The Past 7:20
   A. Approval of Minutes
   B. Report of Sports Camp
   C. Approval of Honorariums for Youth Rally
   D. Report of Evangelism Workshop

II. Realizing The Present 7:50
   A. Devotion-Reflection

III. Preparing For The Future 8:10
   A. Sponsorship of Junior High Summer Camp
   B. Leadership Development Workshops
   C. Work Area Chair Reports
   D. Calendar Building

Adjournment 9:15

Whatever format works best for a particular religious education meeting, it remains important to distribute the printed agenda well in advance of the meeting time.

An Acknowledged Conflict

The Jerusalem circumstances from Acts 6 point to an internal conflict which prompted the meeting and subsequent discussion. It seems obvious that conflict served the important function of ultimately enhancing the program.

By contrast, modern religious meetings often operate with an "avoid conflict at all cost" mentality. One religious education volunteer spoke with pride, "We've never had a split vote in our meetings. Our committee is totally unified." While unity may possibly explain the phenomenon, it seems more likely that people just do not feel free to speak up and voice alternative views.

Researchers in the development of small groups for decision making agree that such groups develop through several phases. Robert Bales described this development as having two phases: formation and production. Those who followed began to raise questions as to how groups might come more quickly to the production phase. As a result, experts recognized several other phases. While they used different names, B. Aubrey Fisher's labels for the phases have become standard terms for the phases of group development. He identified four phases of group development:

1. Orientation
2. Conflict
3. Emergence
4. Reinforcement

In the orientation phase, group members focus on the reason for their existence as a body. The roles of particular members may be established, as well as the norms by which the group will operate.

In the conflict phase, the emergence of difference of opinion and the positioning for persuasive power develop. Under ideal conditions this conflict, rather than being destructive or negative, fosters a spirit of cooperative competition.

In the emergence phase, one position begins to emerge as the best among all alternatives. Sometimes criteria for testing various concepts must be established before emergence can occur. At other times, these criteria enjoy consensus without verbal expression.

Finally, the reinforcement phase hosts an intense, almost exaggerated spirit of unity and cooperation among group members. Statements of loyalty to group members and decisions characterize this phase.

Small group researchers maintain that without intervention by the leadership, groups will over time pass through each of the four phases. It is further generally agreed that groups seldom skip from one stage to another. For example, B. W. Tuckman, who labeled the stages forming, storming, norming, and performing, argued that without the storming phase a group cannot maximize its performing potential.

This research points to the notion that healthy conflict ought to be viewed as a positive aspect of group decision making. While stirring up trouble at the religious education volunteers meeting proves less than productive, avoiding the "flight" mentality with regard to natural differences of opinion may ultimately aid in total group performance.

Procedural Effectiveness

From Acts 6 we know that the Apostles made a proposal for solution of the program problem. One speech in favor of the proposal appears in verses 3 and 4. A statement of consensus by the whole group characterizes verse 5. It seems clear from the flow of the text that the body operated in a manner that proved procedurally effective.

In today's religious education meetings, subtle modifications in established rules of order often reduce effectiveness. Many times discussion develops to the point of consensus, which is in turn followed by a motion and a vote.

Bales labeled this process "fantasy chain." The fantasy chain develops when someone mentions a resonant theme to which others in the group respond. Soon discussion, marked by increased interaction speed, louder voices, and nonverbal cues of excitement, has created a kind of group legend or story. The chain often continues until the theme has been totally exhausted.

By contrast, established rules of order insist that discussion flow from a particular motion. Far from confining group discussion, this important restraint channels thinking and allows every proposed solution to be fairly addressed. When a fantasy chain threatens to divert group attention from the real business at hand, the motion brings the group back to the business at hand.

Uncertainty provides one clue as to why religious education administrators sometimes fail to follow established rules of order. Yet it is vitally important that the religious education administrator lead along the lines of Robert's or some other rules of order. These allow the business to be conducted with maximum efficiency and optimal input from all participants. The chart on the next page summarizes some basics from *Robert's Rules of Order*:

The flow chart is best understood when accompanied by a few basic rules of order. These include:

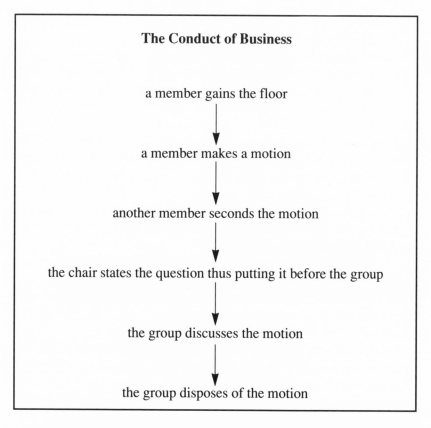

The Conduct of Business

a member gains the floor

a member makes a motion

another member seconds the motion

the chair states the question thus putting it before the group

the group discusses the motion

the group disposes of the motion

1. All main motions must be moved, seconded, discussed, and voted.

2. Voting may be by voice, raised hands, standing, or ballot.

3. Motions may be disposed of by acceptance, rejection, amendment, or postponement.

4. Only the motion at hand may be discussed, but that with full, free, equal time.

5. The leader must remain impartial and fair, while keeping business flowing.

Occasionally a member will wish to amend a main motion currently before the group. In this case, the amendment must be moved and seconded. If after discussion the amendment passes, the amended motion becomes the new order of business for the group.

While this brief overview deals with many questions of procedure, the frequent leader of business meetings will want to obtain a copy of *Robert's* or some other standard rules for order.

All of this attention to rules of order leading to a vote does not rule out the possibility of operating by consensus. Em Griffin suggests that effectiveness in consensus operation requires:

1. Announcing in advance that the body will operate by consensus. That lets participants know that it is necessary to convince everyone.

2. Process orientation. Reaching consensus requires much more time to process input than simply hearing speeches "for" and "against" prior to a vote.

3. Encouraging disagreement. In consensus operation, everyone must be free to speak up. Often the leader will need to probe for the true feelings.

4. Toleration of silence. Silence is not necessarily agreement. It may indicate fear of speaking out.

5. Accepting compromise. Consensus usually will not be gained by everyone approving one plan or the other. Often both sides must sacrifice a portion of their position.

Divisions of Labor

The basis of the proposal advanced by the Twelve in the Jerusalem meeting lies in the concept of division of labor. In effect the group decision empowers a new committee to operate on its behalf.

Today, the best approach to religious education recognizes the importance of a division of labor. Sometimes, especially small membership churches express reluctance to utilize committees to accomplish the task. A general feeling prevails that empowering a small group to enact business diminishes the authority of all others.

Griffin suggests that one of the key ways for a group to make a decision is to appoint an expert, thus dividing the labor into its smallest component. He further notes that while the efficiency of such a procedure is high, the effectiveness may be questionable. However, utilizing committees multiplies the entire group's ability to perform. Of course, committees should not be given free reign over total-group matters but held accountable through regular reports to the body. Often, the total group will want to vote to accept the report of a subgroup, thus maintaining a reminder of authority.

Divine Oversight

Once a committee had been elected by the Jerusalem group, a time of prayer and "sending forth" followed. In fact the word "apostle" literally means one who is sent forth. Earlier, as well, the meeting noted the need for the committee members to be empowered by the Spirit. These factors combine to point to an attitude of Divine oversight.

Too frequently, modern religious education meetings leave volunteer participants with the notion that the task and its accomplishments are effectively separate and distinct from the spiritual dimension of the church. Elements like a time of prayer or devotion included in the meeting, as well as commissioning members ceremonially to new tasks, all enhance the spiritual dimension of the business meeting.

Accurate Record Keeping

Presumably records were made of the Jerusalem meeting which launched the program for ministering to widows and orphans. Whether they were oral or written, they did suffice to document the activities for nearly 2000 years.

Accurate minutes of proceedings increase the efficiency of future group deliberations and decisions. Minutes may be mailed in advance (perhaps with the agenda) of the next meeting, or read for approval. The minutes should include:

1. Identification data such as group name, chair, kind of meeting, date, place, and time.
2. A list of members present or absent.
3. A running account of activities, motives, discussions, and decisions.
4. The signature of the one making the minutes.

A careful examination of the important and historic meeting recorded in Acts 6:1-7 reveals several keys to making meetings with modern religious education volunteers more effective. Perhaps implementation of these keys will yield similar results. "So the word of God spread. The number of disciples in Jerusalem increased rapidly, and a large number of priests became obedient to the faith" (Acts 6:7 NIV).

For Further Reading

Bales, Robert F. *Interaction Process Analysis*. Reading, Mass.: Addison-Wesley, 1950.

Fisher, B.Aubrey. *Small Group Decision Making*. New York: McGraw-Hill, 1974.

Griffin, Em. *Getting Together*. Downers Grove, Ill.: InterVarsity, 1982.

Robert, General Henry M. *Robert's Rules of Order Newly Revised*. Glenview, Ill.: Scott, Foresman, 1970.

Tuckman, B.W. "Developmental Sequences in Small Groups." *Psychological Bulletin* 63 (1965), pp. 384-399.

Chapter Twenty-Two

Communicating with Volunteers

People in the modern world are obsessed with the concept of communication. Colleges and universities scramble to add courses in communication. Salespeople accept communication as the key to effective retailing. Today's business heads expect leaders who will do more than just give orders: They must communicate. Husbands and wives hear repeated counsel that quality communication forms the basis for marital success. Popular magazines feature numerous "how to" articles on communication.

In response to the obsession, one may logically question, "Why a chapter on communicating with volunteers? Doesn't it follow that since people comprise the work force, those who communicate effectively with other people have no trouble communicating with volunteers?"

The answer lies first in exploring the nature of organizational communication. An organization is a system of interdependent and interrelated parts. Hence the religious education program is an organization. These parts may include departments, committees, or work units, but, most of all, people make up organizational systems. Maximizing the interrelatedness of these parts causes the organization to function most effectively. Such maximization occurs through communication.

For example, a manufacturing organization requires an interrelatedness between the sales staff, engineering, and the production department. The organization operates at peak effectiveness only when:

1. Sales communicates customer needs to engineering and orders to production.
2. Production communicates manufacturing problems to engineering and production quota capabilities to sales.
3. Engineering communicates manufacturing technology to production and design capabilities to sales.

But imagine the sales unit in this hypothetical organization composed entirely of volunteers. The interrelatedness which stems from effective communication may now become much more difficult. The volunteer sales people may work unusual or inconsistent hours, resulting in their never seeing the personnel of the other departments. Further, the production and engineering staff composed of paid professionals may see the volunteer sales force as inferior and thus not worthy of communication time. Eventually the volunteer sales force will undoubtedly become ineffective in their work and inefficient in their use of time as a result of the expectations of the other departments of the organization. Unfortunately, in the midst of these difficulties, management may address the problems saying, "After all, they're only volunteers."

While manufacturing organizations avoid the use of an all-volunteer sales force, the problems it might create offer no surprise to the typical religious education organization. Those groups know all too well the issues involved in communicating with volunteers in order to enhance their interrelatedness with the rest of the organization. Four keys to improving communication with volunteers will assist in that process.

1. Create a Spirit of Belonging

A religious education volunteer working in a youth camp advised her pastor of her intention to quit her once-a-week, four-hour shift. "I like the work," she lamented, "but I just don't fit in there anymore."

Earlier examination had revealed the need to revamp the camp's entire volunteer program. The changes that had been made appeared minor, yet they threatened to overwhelm one woman's spirit of volunteerism. The real problem stemmed from the camp administrator's failure to consult the one person, a volunteer, most impacted by the change.

Since God first looked upon Adam and declared, "It is not good for man to be alone," human beings have searched for a place to belong. Volunteers, far from being the exception, may in fact volunteer in order to fulfill their inner need to belong. These same volunteers often feel excluded from those organizational activities which would best meet that need.

While a large team of religious education volunteers, perhaps comprising an entire organizational division, usually integrates effectively into the life of the system, a lone volunteer working alongside paid staff may continue to feel isolated.

The effective manager of religious education volunteers will want to foster the spirit of belonging whenever possible. A partial list of techniques below may provoke thinking toward that end.

1. Include volunteers in staff picnics and/or parties.
2. Provide volunteers with an intraorganizational mailbox.
3. List volunteers in staff telephone and address directories.
4. Include volunteers when routing open memos to the organization.
5. Invite volunteers to sit in on committee meetings where the agenda will encompass their work area.
6. Publicly recognize volunteers periodically for work accomplishments and/or tenure.
7. Encourage volunteers to participate in staff luncheons and other social/business activities.
8. Consciously search for other opportunities to create in volunteers a spirit of belonging to the organization.

2. Consider the Volunteer Perspective

Ask two witnesses to the same traffic mishap to describe the sequence of events. Two very different reports will likely result. Both intend to tell the truth, and both believe in the accuracy of their report. The differences lie in perspective.

Someone has suggested that perspective structures reality. While most people lack a clear ability to determine objective reality, they will accept as truth their own point of view. Often, communication breaks down between volunteers and their managers because the latter fails to consider the volunteer perspective.

One priest reported a serious communication breakdown between the religious education committee of the church and the all-volunteer parish teaching staff. The problem began when the religious education committee decided to institute a CCD elective program on a trial basis. From the committee's perspective, the idea seemed positive. Why not try any new technique with the potential to enhance the educational ministry of the church?

Volunteers on the other hand viewed the move as a threat to their religious education ministry. They had become comfortable and effective in the age level classes. Why disrupt everything just to try some new idea?

In short, the problem stemmed from opposing perspectives. The committee and the teachers did not view the change from the same point of view. In this, as in many similar cases, board members might have averted the problem had they considered the volunteer perspective.

Of course, such perspective problems can exist between two groups or individuals who comprise the paid professional staff of an organization. There seems, however, to exist a general viewpoint unique to volunteers.

Elements of the volunteer perspective include:

1. *A high view of the organization.* Generally volunteers have selected one organization over all others as the best place to offer their services. While this selection may stem from a match between personal skills with organizational needs, often the selection process focuses on the relative merits of the organization. Frequently, volunteers clash perspectives with paid employees who see the organization as "just a place to work."

2. *A low view of personal skills.* One need only reflect upon the description "I'm just a volunteer" to conclude that often volunteers see themselves as inferior to the paid staff. Perhaps the materialistic mentality which measures success in terms of earning power has fed the notion that no pay stems from low worth to the organization. At any rate, the low view of self, when incorporated into the volunteer perspective, must be addressed by managers.

3. *A conviction of the need.* The volunteer seemingly has internally integrated a high view of the organization with a low view of personal skills and concluded, "While this is an outstanding organization, and I have little to offer; one area does exist where I can help meet an organizational need." In short, the volunteer has discovered a place of need in at least one aspect of the total organizational purpose. The wise manager will want to affirm the volunteer in the fulfillment of that role.

3. Listen

Two small children visited the Sunday school classroom. One of the pair was obviously concerned about something. "What's bothering you?" inquired his friend.

"It's my mom," came the response. "I'm worried about her because she talks to herself."

"Don't worry," shot back the first. "Our Sunday school teacher talks to herself, too. She thinks the whole class is listening."

The humor of the exchange fades when we consider that the volunteer religious educator probably sensed that students were not listening. In fact, that teacher may recognize that others in the organization do not take volunteers seriously enough to really listen. Like so many volunteers, this teacher may long for an organization that takes seriously its commitment to volunteers through "full faculty hearing," focused attention, and attempting to understand. "Full faculty hearing" recognizes that hearing and listening are not synonymous terms. Often we associate listening with the physiological process of using the ears. While a connection exists between listening and hearing, effective listening involves all of the senses and faculties, not just the ears.

A religious education volunteer may, for example, communicate a great deal through physical appearance on the job, quality of work, or the willingness or avoidance of eye contact with paid co-workers. The effective manager of volunteers will want to listen carefully to all these communiques and respond to each appropriately.

Focused attention relates to full faculty hearing. Each day, bombarded with sounds ranging from the demands of children to the lure of advertisers, potential listeners effectively tune out a great deal. Those who work with volunteers are no exception. In fact, unconsciously, some seem to feel that one acceptable place to rest attention receptors is when volunteers attempt to communicate.

"Attempting to understand" adequately labels the third phase of the listening process. Some Native Americans use an expression which loosely translated invites, "Walk a mile in my moccasins." That concept characterizes good listening. Managers of volunteers benefit from a constant, silent use of the why questions. "Why are my volunteers doing this? Why is this an issue now? Why did this person volunteer in the first place?"

These three phases—full faculty hearing, paying close attention, and attempting to understand—enhance the listening side of communication in all settings. When applied to work with volunteers, they further enhance volunteer/manager relationship.

4. Search for Effective Media

Carol had always volunteered to help with the luncheon provided by her local church for bereaved families on the day of the funeral. At one such function, however, Carol did not appear. Later, it was learned that in response to a family budget crunch, Carol and her husband had discontinued the daily paper. News of the death and church luncheon had failed to reach her, hence the church lost a valuable volunteer for this important ministry.

The problem of Carol, and many religious education volunteers like her, could be avoided if the organization had chosen more effective media by which to communicate with its volunteers. In some circumstances, the evening paper might be an appropriate medium. In other cases, like Carol's, leaders must search for a more effective way to get out the word. Often volunteers work inconsistent hours or perform their duties off-site. For example, a Sunday school teacher usually prepares lessons at home without the direct supervision of a supervisor. These circumstances compound the medium selection process.

While selection of the appropriate communication medium will necessarily be unique to each organization and team of volunteers, the list of potential channels below may stimulate thinking.

1. Volunteer staff meetings
2. Volunteer newsletters
3. On-site volunteer mailboxes
4. Telephone chains
5. Volunteer bulletin boards
6. Posters
7. Announcements in the church bulletin
8. Video updates at a central location

Just as no one medium will serve every communication need, so no one key to improving communication with volunteers will perfect every situation. Managers must, however, recognize the unique features of communicating with volunteers in order to maximize the potential of this great human asset.

For Further Reading

Morrison, Emily. *Skills for Leadership: Working with Volunteers*, vol. 1. Tucson, Ariz.: Jordan, 1988.

Wilson, Marlene. *The Effective Management of Volunteer Programs*. Boulder, Colo.: Volunteer Management Association, 1976.

Wolvin, Andrew, and Carolyn Gwynn Coakley. *Listening*, 3rd ed. Dubuque: Brown, 1988.

Chapter Twenty-Three

Solving Volunteer Problems

"Pastor," Angela spoke cautiously, "I'm afraid I have to resign as coordinator of children's religious education. I've held the job for seven years."

"And have done a marvelous job," interrupted Pastor Steele.

"But," Angela continued, "I'm just worn out. I don't seem to have the new, fresh ideas required to do the job right."

After Angela left, Pastor Steele slumped into his office chair to contemplate. She represented the third serious problem this week with the volunteer religious education ministry of his mid-sized church. On Monday a rift between two of the teachers in the children's religious education program had come to his attention. It seems that the co-workers had carried a neighborhood dispute into the church. The pair continued to function in their respective roles, but even the elementary age children had noticed the strain.

Then, only yesterday the coordinator of youth ministry came bearing the news that one of the junior high advisors had failed to keep a commitment to chaperone the rock-a-thon. Parents were understandably up in arms that teens spent the first night of the event without an adult presence.

Even though Pastor Steele and other coordinators of volunteers function as effectively as possible, problems still arise. The most effective planning, training, administering, supervising, and evaluating will never anticipate and avoid all volunteer problems. Usually, these problems fit into three broad categories:

1. Personal problems
2. Interpersonal problems
3. Performance problems

This chapter seeks to consider each of the three.

Personal Problems

Since Herbert Freudenberger and Geraldine Richelson first coined the term "burnout," it has become one of the most popular expressions of modern culture. Usually burnout refers to depression from job-related fatigue, often because rewards of a given task do not provide adequate renewal. Angela, from the opening illustration of this chapter, may be suffering burnout.

Donald Demaray suggests that while all of us experience, from time to time, the characteristics of burnout, chronic weariness requires attention. Frustration, boredom, depression, hopelessness, stress, and irritability may all signal a burnout problem. Ironically, those volunteers who have given the most dedicated service may be most susceptible to burnout.

One outstanding book dealing with solutions to burnout focuses on clergy renewal. However, David McKenna's approach can be readily applied to religious education volunteers. He suggests that renewal comes through a twelve-step process.

The first step, "reliving our call," involves remembering for whom we volunteered as religious educators in the first place. We developed the concept of divine summons in chapter eighteen. Allowing volunteers to express that original motivation in a public forum from time to time assists in reliving the call. Time might be provided in a church service, Sunday school, or prayer meeting for this purpose.

McKenna offers as a second step to renewal, "remembering our commitment." Here the focus shifts to purpose. The "why" of religious education volunteerism needs to be addressed frequently. Keep the program goals before the volunteers to minimize the burnout syndrome. One church kept those goals fresh (and participated in an ongoing evaluation) by circulating a questionnaire about previously agreed-upon goals.

"Reclaiming our promise" encapsulates McKenna's third step. Religious education volunteers must recognize that human strength alone is not enough for the tremendous task of religious education. God promises support and strength. Volunteers should be encouraged to spend much time in prayer, meditation, and Bible reading in order to tap this reservoir of resources.

To maintain motivation we must "respect our differences," McKenna suggests. All religious education volunteers will not function effectively in every task. Effective screening (chapter ten) helps avoid burnout problems arising from this important factor."

Regaining our balance, McKenna suggests, involves the development of a healthy blend of leisure time with task time. Single issue people burn out the fastest. One church built a minivacation into their religious education volunteers' lives by declaring every fifth Sunday as substitute Sunday. Another developed an elective program for summer months to give age level teachers a breather.

These built-in sabbaticals also relate well to McKenna's sixth step to renewal, "recycling our resources." Churches which recognize the valuable resource of lay religious education volunteers will want to provide means whereby those resources are renewed and replenished. Such events as seminars or classes for credit paid for by the church provide a forum for renewal.

McKenna suggests "remembering our servanthood" as also crucial to personal renewal. Jesus clearly taught his volunteers the similarity of leadership and service. Those who volunteer to lead and hence to serve are less likely to meet with disappointing results. One religious education leader from a denomination which practices the sacrament of foot-washing humbled himself before his volunteers in the performance of that ceremony. Leaders have discovered other ways to place themselves in servant roles.

McKenna argues for renewal from "rebuilding our leadership" as an eighth step. Application of our discussion on the principles of delegation (chapter five) helps to spread the volunteer workload between a number of likely candidates.

"Regulating the task" prevents burnout by recognizing that all volunteers do not hold inherent capabilities for every task. One church applied this principle by limiting to one the number of volunteer tasks any member could address at any particular time. Not only did the result prevent burnout in a few, it encouraged the involvement of many.

McKenna suggests "recognizing our limits" as an important regulatory task in the control of burnout. A volunteer in evangelism received sound advice when told, "You won't reach everyone. Set a reasonable goal and work toward that." The reasonable goals for religious education volunteers in general are considered in chapter six.

The issue of accountability comes into focus in McKenna's chapter on "reporting our results." Religious education volunteers responsible to no one seldom receive the kind of encouragement and definition necessary to prevent burnout.

Finally, McKenna suggests "redeeming our future" as an important step in renewal. Putting the new wine of 1990s needs into the old wineskins of existing religious education programs undoubtedly yields stressful, burned out volunteers. Tailoring the approach of the volunteer program to today's "market" helps relieve those tensions.

Of course, burnout represents only one, albeit common, example of a personal problem that can interfere with a volunteer's religious education ministry. The successful coordinator of volunteers must regularly cope with problems of family, finance, grief, jobs, and physical health since these issues threaten religious education volunteer performance. Further, most coordinators lack the professional skills necessary to professionally counsel in any of these areas.

Gary Collins offers six principles which are important to those who intend to help peers through problems, yet find themselves lacking professional training in counseling. He first advises the people-helper to remember that the personality, values, attitudes, and beliefs of the helper are of primary importance. Having a caring spirit goes a long way in overcoming professional limitations.

A second Collins principle reminds helpers that the helpee's attitudes, motivation, and desire to help are also important. Volunteer coordinators may discover their need for help in providing more motivation to solve problems than the helpee possesses. A basic rule contends, "You cannot help those who don't want help."

Principle three offered by Collins focuses on the relationship between the helper and the helpee. Coordinators of religious education volunteers will find the greatest success in helping with personal problems when the helping is a product of an ongoing relationship with the volunteer. The time to begin relationship building is long before a crisis appears.

Collins declares in principle four that emotions, thoughts, and behaviors are all intertwined together as the focus of the most effective helping. Simply patching up problems in order to get volunteers back to work falls short of the people helping mark.

As a fifth principle in people helping, Collins warns against single-technique approaches. Some circumstances require careful listening, others directive advising, still others the presentation of options.

The sixth principle offered by Collins points to the ultimate goal of helping which is making disciples and disciplers. The coordinator of religious education volunteers who limits the task of people helping to getting volunteers functionally able to perform religious education duties falls far short of the opportunities for ministry.

Interpersonal Problems

Often the problems which religious education volunteers encounter could best be characterized as interpersonal instead of personal. Problems which grow out of the relationship between a particular volunteer and someone else in the organization we term interpersonal problems. Often such problems dissolve simply with a brief discussion. At other times they threaten the stability of the entire religious education program. In chapter eighteen we discussed organizational conflict in the context of asking some volunteers to leave. In some cases, however, basic steps to interpersonal conflict resolution will help.

First, acknowledge the conflict. Often religious organizations tend to ignore interpersonal squabbles, believing that harmony provides the only appropriate public witness. Such flight from reality, however, does nothing to aid interpersonal growth, or get the volunteer organization on track. As an important part of the acknowledgment step, the manager of volunteers will want to accurately determine the nature of the conflict. Is the problem issue-oriented, or do two volunteers just have a personality clash? The solution may well lie in the answer to that question.

Second, the resolver of conflict will want to consider personal feelings toward combatants or the circumstances. A religious education volunteer coordinator who is biologically related to one of the persons in conflict, for example, may need additional help in maintaining objectivity. Similarly, a deep personal interest in the outcome of issues may create rather than alleviate difficult circumstances.

Third, keep the focus on the real issues. Often, participants in an interpersonal squabble will tend toward personal attack rather than issue-oriented discussion. The manager of conflict will maximize success by listening carefully for indications of ego-involvement such as slanderous innuendoes.

Fourth, explore several possible solutions. Most interpersonal conflict has more than one potential solution. Facilitating combatants as they explore several of these is a key role of the conflict manager. At this stage, it will also prove necessary to make sure both sides of a question receive a fair hearing. One person withdrawing without being truly convinced does not provide a solution but only a return to the original state.

Finally, assure implementation. Once a course of action which solves the issues of conflict emerges, the manager of conflict will need to oversee the process of putting that solution in place. The implementation must be accomplished without sacrificing the feelings or reputation of either conflict participant.

While no guarantee exists in the volatile area of interpersonal conflict, these five keys do minimize the possibility of long term disruption.

Performance Problems

Performance problems constitute the final area requiring consideration under the general rubric of volunteer problems. Sometimes, even in the absence of off-the-job personal problems, or on-the-job interpersonal problems, volunteers fail to accomplish the assigned tasks. Late arrival, shoddy work, high absenteeism, or incomplete assignments all fall into this category.

Generally, performance problems fit into one of two broad classifications.

1. Problems of motivation
2. Problems of training

Chapters seventeen and thirteen respectively deal with these two areas, because they are more supervisory than administrative issues. Often, however, the volunteer religious education administrator will find it difficult to determine whether a particular performance problem requires training or motivational input. At this point an administrator might suggest the use of the performance evaluation analysis illustrated below.

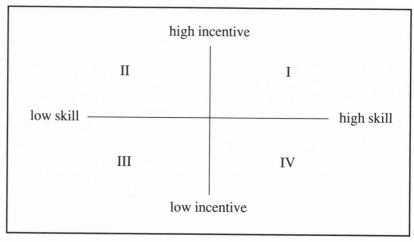

As the administrator or supervisor analyzes a particular performance problem, a rating on two scales, skill and incentive, becomes necessary. Plotting the ratings yields one of four quadrants. For example, a volunteer known to possess ability (high skill) but not stimulated to perform (low incentive) appears in quadrant IV. Similarly, low skill and low incentive yield quadrant III, while a volunteer who tries very hard but lacks skills appears in quadrant II. Once the appropriate quadrant has been identified, solutions can be prescribed from an appropriate mixture of motivational therapy and training.

Performance Evaluation Guide

Quadrant	Solution
I	none necessary
II	training
III	training and motivation
IV	motivation

Pastor Steele, from the opening illustration, clearly faces a volunteer problem in each of the three categories explored in this chapter: personal, interpersonal, and performance. As with other coordinators of volunteers, Pastor Steele will find continuing challenges in the implementation of solutions. The ideas in this chapter may be a starting point for resolving such difficulties.

For Further Reading

Collins, Gary. *How To Be a People Helper*. Ventura, Calif.: Regal, 1976.

Demaray, Donald E. *Watch Out For Burnout*. Grand Rapids, Mich.: Baker, 1983.

Freudenberger, Herbert J., and Geraldine Richelson. *Burnout: The High Cost of High Achievement*. Garden City, N.Y.: Doubleday, 1981.

McKenna, David L. *Renewing Our Ministry*. Waco, Tex.: Word, 1986.

Part VII

Evaluating
Religious Education
Volunteer Programs

Chapter Twenty-Four

Evaluating the Results of Volunteer Programs

Someone has suggested that the epitaph of the church will read, "We never did it that way before." For many congregations, those words represent the only evaluation a potential new program ever receives. "If we've gotten by without a planning retreat for all these years, why start that now?" Existing programs receive even less evaluation: "If we held a Vacation Bible School last year, of course we'll have one this year."

As we noted earlier, however, evaluation encompasses one of the key functions of administration. John Cionca in his functional book, *The Trouble-Shooting Guide to Christian Education*, suggests three concerns for regular evaluation:

1. Facilities
2. Program
3. Teachers

This chapter will focus on the second of these assessment needs. The third, teachers, we considered in chapter fourteen. Before exploring procedures for a comprehensive evaluation of the religious education program, an examination of several ongoing areas requiring evaluation may prove beneficial.

Volunteer Turnover

One measure of the effectiveness of a program lies in how comfortably people work within that program. A high volunteer turnover may indicate some problem needs addressing by administrators. Further, one religious education program which encompasses a higher turnover rate than others points to a potential problem.

Recognizing a high religious education volunteer turnover, and thus a possible program problem, provides only a portion of the information needed for effective evaluation. Locating the problem or underlying cause of high turnover might best be accomplished in exit interviews.

A large percentage of industrial organizations use an exit interview during the final days of employment in order to determine why employees leave. While the exit interview of the religious education program will usually be less formal, a wide array of information can be gleaned. Topics to cover during the course of the interview include:

1. Reasons for leaving the task
2. Relationship with program leadership
3. Relationship with other volunteers
4. Evaluation of overall ministry
5. Most positive aspects of program
6. Most negative aspects of program
7. Volunteer's suggestions

Budgetary Considerations

Most religious organizations compile a monthly report of income and expenditures. This document provides an excellent source of information for the administrator interested in program evaluation and willing to ask difficult questions about the return on investment for each program.

Religious organizations might dismiss questions concerning fiscal return as less than spiritual. While it is true that the religious education program of the church targets a purpose far higher than a simple profit motive, it is also true that good stewardship requires the most effective use of program dollars.

One local church religious education board, when viewing the expenditures for summer children's camp, believed that outlay to be very high for the degree of religious education effectiveness. Their opinion prompted deeper investigation which revealed a large portion of the money was paid for craft kits which did not effectively teach the lesson. A retired church member volunteered to make up kits which related to the Bible at a fraction of the retail cost. A further advantage lay in the fact that the do-it-yourself kits could be designed to better relate to teacher-developed lesson material. Hence, a simple budget review led to program evaluation and correction.

Comparison Evaluation

Livestock breeders know that dangers of enhancing the poorest qualities exist when stock is inbred for several generations. To avoid the problem, new animals are introduced into the herd from time to time. Similarly, the religious education program which evaluates only itself and which develops and trains its own volunteers over long periods of time may discover itself perpetuating some less than effective training measures. On the other hand, exposure to other programs, procedures, and personnel tends to enhance performance.

Several small-membership local churches sent representatives to a denominationally sponsored Vacation Bible School director's workshop. The workshop, which brought together several dozen V.B.S. leaders, provided new concepts which ultimately upgraded the programs of many. Returning to her local congregation, one director declared, "Before this, I just assumed everyone did it the same way we did."

In addition to denominational gatherings, sources for such comparison evaluation include:

1. Workshops by local religious education professionals
2. Community groups of clergy
3. Curriculum publisher's workshops
4. Religious bookstore seminars
5. Casual neighborhood dialogue
6. New members from other churches or communities
7. Visitors

In each case, comparison evaluation has the advantage of allowing evaluation and correction prior to need recognition. Volunteers more willingly adopt a new idea when the traditional procedure has undergone scrutiny and been found wanting.

Attitude Surveys

Attitude surveys generally involve the use of a questionaire which invites participants to declare their opinions on certain topics. Not only might attitude surveys be used with the volunteers conducting a program, but with the program participants as well.

The design of the attitude survey will depend on several factors:

1. The goal of the program
2. The role of the survey participant in the program
3. The frequency of survey administration
4. The time available to complete the survey

The samples on the next page show several ways to approach the same attitudinal information.

Example #1

This religious education elective met my expectations.(check one)

yes   no   uncertain

Example #2

This religious education elective met my expectations.(circle one)

1   2   3   4   5
expectations   expectations
totally unmet   totally met

Example #3

This religious education elective met my expectations

(mark the appropriate place on the line)

expectations   expectations
totally unmet   totally met

Whatever style instrument the administrator of a volunteer program selects, careful planning and administering of the instrument must be followed up by analyzing the data and taking appropriate action. Communication changes resulting from the input of participants in the survey increases the incentive to assist with such evaluation in the future.

Brainstorming Follow-up

A final technique which often proves useful as an evaluative tool might best be described as brainstorming follow-up. The technique works best as an evaluation for infrequent, one-of-a-kind type events as compared to ongoing and regular programs. The process involves bringing all the personnel from an event together to ask three basic questions.

1. What did we do well?
2. What needs improvement?
3. How could we do better?

These simple questions, addressed individually by the group as a whole, often yield bountiful results.

One key to the success of such evaluation lies in enforcing the notion that no right or wrong opinions exist at the brainstorming stage. Further, if minds wander to tangentially related programs or topics, the evaluation, far from being lost, may prove even more beneficial.

A very small, rural church attempted for the first time an intergenerational Vacation Bible School. The program design included a brief devotion and singing followed by a lesson-related craft wherein adults assisted teens who, in turn, assisted children. During the craft period, the devotional lesson was discussed and memory verses practiced. After the one week V.B.S., volunteers anxiously came together to participate in a brainstorming follow-up. Items noted during their discussion included:

I. What did we do well?
   1. Blended the old and young in a joint study
   2. Organized events
   3. Provided a lovely useful craft that related well to the Bible lesson
   4. Involved both men and women in teaching
   5. Saved teacher preparation time by using a single devotion for all ages.
II. What needs improvement?
   1. Songs and choruses didn't match lesson theme
   2. Refreshment time was disruptive
   3. First night confusion in assigning craft groups
   4. One person got stuck with clean-up
   5. Leaders didn't have printed copies of memory verses
   6. Students played close to road after program
III. What could we do better?
   1. To solve item #1 above
      A) Provide lesson material to musicians in advance
      B) Incorporate songs in lesson rather than in an opening exercise
   2. To solve item #2 above
      A) Move refreshment time to the end of craft section
   3. To solve item #3 above
      A) Use a preregistration system
      B) Have adult leader work on assignment to groups of those not pre-registered during first night devotion.

    4. To solve item #4 above

       A) Ask each group to clean up after crafts and before refreshments

       B) Appoint clean-up committee to follow-up

       C) Get trash barrel on the site

    5. To solve item #5 above

       A) Run off memory verses in advance for every participant

    6. To solve item #6 above

       A) Develop organized postmeeting games

       B) Appoint adult to monitor busy highway

       C) Ask highway crews for "children playing" signs

As with any brainstorming activity, this example clearly shows a tendency to ramble from one aspect to another of the evaluation. On the other hand, there appears to be clear evidence of group involvement in the evaluative task, followed by a definite plan for follow-up action.

Comprehensive Evaluation

The ongoing evaluative processes discussed thus far, while helpful to most religious education programs, fall short of the benefits derived from comprehensive evaluations. Comprehensive evaluation examines the total religious education program of a church in one appraisal.

Harold Westing in the appendix to his book, *Evaluate and Grow*, offers four self-study guides which combine to accomplish a comprehensive evaluation. He divides the study into guides for:

    1. Preschool departments

    2. Grade school departments

    3. Youth departments

    4. Adult departments

Each of the four guides considers such departmental functions as:

    1. Preparations

    2. Organization

    3. Class session

    4. Relationships

    5. Teacher's role

    6. Scheduling

    7. Student development

    8. Facilities

Appraisers evaluate the religious education program by checking either improvement needed, started, or progress for each of a series of evaluative statements.

While Westing's suggestions act as an excellent starting point for the evaluator of a religious education program, each appraiser will want to tailor forms and procedures to the specific task. The one common element in all such evaluative measures, however, lies at the point of beginning. Only frustration can result from evaluating a religious education program which lacks a sufficiently clear goal. As someone has quipped, "If you don't know where you're going, you get there every time."

Having firmly established program goals, the evaluation seeks to determine to what degree the religious education program meets these goals. The evaluator will need to consider at least:

1. Do facilities make reaching the goal possible?
2. Are teachers properly trained and motivated to the goal?
3. Are the volunteer personnel acquainted with and supportive of the program goals?
4. Is the goal being accomplished?
5. Does the professional staff understand and support the goals?
6. Do curriculum materials aim at the accomplishment of the program goals?

Clearly no one instrument or interview will answer all of these questions in a comprehensive manner. Instead, the comprehensive evaluation combines surveys, interviews, and observations over time into one report.

The question of who should conduct the comprehensive evaluation must be addressed early in the process. Some churches choose a religious education director or other person within the organization, either volunteer or professional, for the task. Advantages to the in-house selection include first-hand knowledge of the program and the possibility of long-term study and comparisons. Persons from outside the organization could be used for tabulation prior to analysis.

Other groups, however, choose to hire an outside consultant to perform the comprehensive evaluation. Advantages to this procedure include a heightened objectivity since the appraiser has no ego-involvement in any aspect of the program. The obvious disadvantage, cost, may be dealt with by two neighboring churches performing the evaluative process for one another on an exchange basis.

Whoever performs the comprehensive evaluation will need to write the results, analysis, and recommendations in a study report. This report should have wide circulation in the entire church, since some problems may be solved by, as yet unrecruited, volunteers.

Whether the religious education department improves by evaluation on an ongoing program-by-program basis, or uses the comprehensive evaluation method, clearly the need for program evaluation cannot be overemphasized. By such methods volunteer, as well as professional, religious educators improve the quality of programs and thus enhance impact in the lives of participants.

For Further Reading

Bannon, William, and Suzanne Donovan. *Volunteers and Ministry*. New York: Paulist, 1983.

Cionca, John R. *The Trouble-Shooting Guide to Christian Education*. Denver: Accent, 1986.

Gangel, Kenneth. *Feeding and Leading*. Wheaton, Ill.: Victor, 1989.

Macduff, Nancy. *Volunteer Recruiting and Retention*. Walla Walla, Wash.: Macduff/Bunt, 1985.

Vineyard, Sue. *Evaluating Volunteers, Programs, and Events*. Downers Grove, Ill.: VMSystems/Heritage Arts, 1988.

Westing, Harold J. *Evaluate and Grow*. Wheaton, Ill.: Victor, 1984.

White, James W. *Intergenerational Religious Education*. Birmingham, Ala.: Religious Education Press, 1988.

Chapter Twenty-Five

Adjusting the Volunteer Program

"If it ain't broke, don't fix it." These words summarized the philosophy of one rather outspoken local religious education director. In his understanding, all change existed only for the sake of change. Perhaps he reacted to the tendency to equate "change" with "progress" among many, including some religious education directors. At any rate, his attitude failed to account for the truth that sometimes program change does serve an effective purpose.

Without evaluation, no valid reasons for change exist. Preceded by adequate objective evaluation, like that described in chapter twenty-four, change may become necessary and even beneficial. In fact, such evaluation leads to only three possible conclusions.

1. The program is presently operating at maximum effectiveness.
2. The present program needs minor modification to increase effectiveness.
3. The present program is dysfunctional.

Some adjustment will be necessary in response to each outcome assessment.

Adjusting the Effective Program

While adjustments to the effective program will be minimal, some "mid-course correction" may still prove helpful. The effective leaders of such a program will want to take necessary steps to help volunteers maintain the cutting edge of their abilities and skills.

Turning the evaluation into a celebration of success causes religious education volunteers to not only recognize success but also contemplate the causes of success. Good evaluation should not become an end, but an ongoing part of the ministry process.

Once the celebration has passed, the tendency to return to the routine of "business as usual" mounts. One religious education director taped a note to herself on her desk. The continuous reminder read, "There is no ordinary Sunday." Herein she found motivation to encourage others to greater levels of success.

Finally, the volunteer program that receives the highest marks in evaluation will want to examine possibilities for expansion. If the goal is being met perfectly, then expansion of the goal may be in order. Could other goals be reached? Is education defined broadly enough? What tools or techniques could help accomplish even more? The leadership of the volunteer program will want to carefully avoid programs for the sake of just having programs. Leadership must first expand vision and overall goal, then tailor programs to fit these.

Adjusting the Less Effective Program

The program evaluation will most frequently yield mixed results. Most volunteer programs in religious education have some very effective aspects, while other portions need improvement. In the presence of such a mixed review, several follow-up evaluative questions emerge. These include:

1. Would more volunteers make the religious education program more effective?
2. Would an increase in volunteer time help?
3. Could the program benefit from an increase in financial or other resources?
4. Have volunteers been trained as fully as possible?
5. Do all volunteers share the task vision?
6. Does the organizational climate support the purpose and mission of the religious education program?
7. Is personnel change, either volunteer or professional, necessary?

Usually the answers to these questions will help draw the focus to the appropriate point of adjustment. Two words of caution:

1. More is not necessarily better. Conventional wisdom often assumes that more money, or more volunteers, or more training will yield more effective results for the religious education program. In fact, the opposite may actually be the case. Reducing a program to a more manageable and accomplishable size often increases overall effectiveness. For example, if a church lacks sufficient volunteers to operate an effective CCD, as well as children's church, the elimination of one or the other may maximize the effectiveness of the programs remaining.

2. Don't "throw out the baby with the bath water." This proverbial

cliche reminds the alert religious education director that mixed results must be handled as just that — mixed. Volunteers who are effective deserve commendation and renewed. This is true even when some elements of the program require adjustment.

Adjusting The Dysfunctional Program

The term "dysfunctional," when applied to the religious education program, stems from David Moberg's sociological analysis of the church. Dysfunctional programs serve the organizational structure, rather than the original need which brought that structure into existence. Furthermore, the efforts to preserve the structure undercut and undermine the original need the structure was intended to meet. This is the meaning of "dysfunctional." For example, a year came when no ninth graders participated in a Sunday school. However, the church advertised the class and appointed a teacher instead of focusing time and effort on actual needs in the educational program. The efforts expended trying to maintain an unneeded class resulted in less energy and motivation toward meeting genuine needs.

When the evaluation process reveals that the program serves the structure instead of the original need, dysfunction may have set in. One church lamented that no one attended the Wednesday evening training program in the summer. When the director of religious education noted the decline and suggested a recess until fall, the religious education committee took decisive action. "The mid-week service will be available," they declared, "in case someone wants to come." The result was that the volunteers wasted precious time that could have been spent in more productive religious education.

Such extreme examples of dysfunctionalism would be funny, did they not represent a tremendous waste of volunteer effort when so much real religious education ministry awaits. Curing dysfunctionalism requires radical changes or total program abandonment. It simply does not work to put "new wine into old wineskins."

Evaluation then will pinpoint the program somewhere on the continuum from effectiveness to dysfunctionalism. Adjustment aims to move the program toward ever-increasing effectiveness.

ADJUSTMENT

Dysfunctional
Program   Effective
Program

All adjustment presupposes change. Change, not being a natural and comfortable element of human existence, requires effective administration. Six approaches to adjustment serve to aid the administrator of the religious education program in the implementation of change.

Cognitive Approach

The cognitive approach to adjustment builds upon the notion that volunteers act upon what they believe. Resistance to adjustment fades as the thinking behind the matter becomes clear.

The director of religious education who wished to adjust the long-standing Vacation Bible School schedule from early morning to evening might use a cognitive approach. Pointing out the sociological transformations which have brought potential teachers to the secular workplace, for example, or noting the possibility of expanding the vision to include an adult class, might cause volunteers to readily accept the adjustment.

Modeling Approach

A modeling approach to adjustment stems from a belief that people act due to the consequences of previous behaviors. In many ways, the approach is the opposite of the cognitive approach. Instead of thought affecting action, consequences impact thought as well as future actions.

One religious education director used this approach to facilitate adjustment in teaching styles in the Sunday school department. Rather than describe better styles of teaching, she began to model those styles in teacher's meetings and then reward imitation with a smile and a compliment. The result, though slow, was pronounced. In other programs, role-playing has helped volunteers to experience improvement, especially when accompanied by social rewards such as attention, clapping, etc.

The use of videotape multiplies the opportunities for modeling in the modern religious education program, as noted in section IV of this book. Now one professional religious educator can demonstrate effective teaching to many volunteer religious educators.

Goals Approach

The goals approach recognizes the fact that volunteers strive to attain goals. Thus, programs become more effective when the standard for success is elevated.

For example, if parish religious educators equate survival with success, then survival becomes the standard. If, on the other hand, assisting youth in the resistance of social pressures becomes the measure of success, a whole new perspective emerges.

Effective leadership involves the total group in the initial establishment of standards. Through the use of positive affirmations, group support for the goal continues to emerge. An impetus of excellence pervades the entire organization.

Role Approach

Adjustment based upon the role approach recognizes that people have certain expectations for certain positions. Adjusting those role norms affects the overall effectiveness of the program.

When job descriptions for teachers in one parish were adjusted, dramatic change occurred. After discussion, teachers accepted, as a part of their volunteer task, the encouragement of student attendance in the class. Whereas they previously saw their role as merely teaching the attenders, they now began to encourage absentees to attend.

Linguistic Approach

Researcher Benjamin Whorf suggests that what we say affects what we do. Adjustment based upon the linguistic approach builds upon this basic truth. James Michael Lee in his *The Content of Religious Education* summarizes this hypothesis and other similar lines of thinking.

In one very small church, the religious education program approached disintegration. The four or five elementary age students shared a class with two or three high schoolers and a half-dozen adults. No one realized much educational benefit from the unusual arrangement. Simply listening to the participants revealed the cause of the problem. "We don't have space for a good program." "We're too small to really have classes." "In the days when this church was thriving, the religious education program was very effective." The key to adjustment in this situation rested in the linguistic approach. Agents of change began to focus conversation and thus attention on what small churches could do better. Phrases like, "We are small enough to really get to know people" and "Small parishes are so much friendlier" were discussed and encouraged. In time, the total program became more effective.

Elimination Approach

Perhaps emotionally the most difficult task for religious education directors is eliminating programs. Often, to eliminate a program is tantamount to failure. On the other hand, George Barna suggests that the most effective churches quickly discard programs that do not produce measurable changes in the lives of people. There are no "sacred cows"; if there is no measurable change due to the program, the program is eliminated. Often, the very act of eliminating a program leads to much more effective total ministry.

One church recognized that its monthly senior citizens' potluck simply was not well enough attended to justify its continuation. Further, it did not accomplish the goals of the religious education program in its present form. The program was dropped. Several religious education volunteers, concerned for the needs of the community's elderly took up the slack with a whole new program of senior adult religious education programs which met at the time of the original social program.

In each of these adjustment approaches, the move toward effectiveness comes gradually. Programs generally do not move from dysfunctional to effective overnight but inch along the continuum of improvement. Failure to begin the adjustment process, however, guarantees failure. Describing the goal can be a first step in reaching that goal.

Instead of the philosophy, "If it ain't broke, don't fix it," quality leadership in the volunteer religious education program declares, "If it ain't working, adjust it or get rid of it."

For Further Reading

Barna, George. *The Frog in the Kettle*. Ventura, Calif.: Regal, 1990.
Barna, George. *User-Friendly Churches*. Ventura, Calif.: Regal, 1991.
Lee, James Michael. *The Content of Religious Education*. Birmingham, Ala.: Religious Education Press, 1985.
Moberg, David O. *The Church as a Social Institution*, 2nd ed. Grand Rapids, Mich.: Baker, 1984.
Sarno, Ronald A. *Using Media in Religious Education*. Birmingham, Ala.: Religious Education Press, 1987.
Whorf, Benjamin. *Language, Thought and Reality*. Cambridge, Mass.: MIT.

Part VIII

Trends and Resources
in Religious Education Volunteerism

Chapter Twenty-Six

Where Is Volunteerism Going?

Predicting the direction of volunteerism for the future requires an analysis of trends related to this topic. Throughout this book we have described a few of these trends as they apply to a specific area of religious education volunteers. Here we will examine these and other trends in detail.

The Megatrends

John Naisbitt, in his 1982 book, evaluated newspaper stories and other media coverage of events and found ten general trends within society. A number of these directly relate to volunteerism and specifically to volunteerism in religious education. The ten trends are marked by movement from:

1. An industrial society to an information society
2. Forced technology to high technology/high touch
3. A national economy to a world economy
4. The short term to the long term
5. Centralization to decentralization
6. Institutional help to self-help
7. Representative democracy to participatory democracy
8. Hierarchies to networking
9. North to South
10. Either/or options to multiple options

While all of these have a bearing upon religious education, particularly the content of religious education efforts, several are crucial for religious education volunteerism in particular.

For example, the "high touch" emphasis in the second megatrend is crucial to religious education volunteerism. Increasingly people want close, personal relationships, because there is less intimacy in modern life, with its emphasis upon productivity and efficiency. Unfortunately the latter have come to be paramount in many churches, as reflected by the overemphasis upon church growth by many church leaders (which often reflects pragmatism more than religious ideals). Volunteer religious education coordinators must assume leadership postures that encourage "high touch" in their relationships with volunteers, with personal encouragement, guidance, and training. In addition, the specific tasks of religious educators should promote "high touch" with those being educated. Perhaps the small group movement in churches reflects the "high touch" Naisbitt describes since personal contact is more likely in the small group context. Most of the megachurches make use of small groups to ensure that "high touch" intimacy supplements the other activities of the church.

The fifth trend, the movement toward decentralization, also has a bearing upon religious education volunteerism. A strong emphasis upon denominational affiliation or upon the institutional church as an organization is unlikely to produce the loyalty it once did. Increasingly people express more interest in religious education volunteerism oriented toward the specific task at hand. Many distrust the centralization implicit in large organizations but appreciate decentralized efforts to accomplish tangible goals.

The trend toward self-help rather than institutional help, again is reflected in the small group movement. Laity are increasingly being seen as an important source of ministry, supplementing that of professionals. The concept of the "priesthood of believers" has long been affirmed in Protestant circles, but actual practice of lay ministry generally has been dormant until the last decade or two. Since Vatican II the concept of lay ministry has also become popular among Roman Catholics. The orientation of self-help, rather than institutional assistance, is reflected in the attitudes of leaders of religious education volunteers as much as specific practices. Realizing the distrust of large organizations, successful religious education volunteer programs will repeatedly emphasize self-help through training, reading, and self-assessment.

Trends seven and eight, participatory democracy and networking, suggest that the best volunteer programs make people feel they have a part in the decisions made. Decentralization in church organization demonstrates this principle, but more specific to religious education volunteerism is for volunteers to directly participate in planning and changes that are made. The move from hierarchy to networking implies that autocratic volunteer leaders and programs are less likely to attract people, but egalitarian "partnership" associations between religious education volunteers (and between volunteers and professionals) needs to take priority. People want to mix and share information on an equal basis. Interestingly Anne Smith's volunteer program stage theory (chapter seven) links excessive bureaucratization with organizational decline and even demise.

The trend toward multiple options is crucial for volunteerism. In the past, potential religious education volunteers have met an either/or approach to volunteerism — either you volunteer for the open position, or do not worry about volunteering at all. Only the tasks designated were available. For religious education volunteerism efforts to be successful in the future, multiple options based upon the needs and abilities of the *volunteer* (not the church organization) are central. We will return to this important factor later in this chapter.

More Megatrends

In 1990 Naisbitt added ten more megatrends to the above list. They include:

1. A global economic boom
2. A renaissance in the arts
3. Free-market socialism
4. Cultural nationalism and global lifestyles
5. Privatization of the welfare state
6. Rise of the Pacific region
7. Women in leadership
8. Age of biology
9. Religious revival
10. Increased individualism

Like his first set of trends, these all have an impact upon religious education. Most significant for volunteerism are the seventh, ninth, and tenth trends.

Women could be counted upon to be religious education volunteers in the past. The ideal of the full-time housewife allowed for more involvement in volunteer efforts, although they often felt imposed upon when church recruiters assumed the stereotype that housewives had little to do with their time. Today, women desire more leadership positions in religious education volunteerism efforts. Men with healthy self-esteem do not feel threatened by leaders who are women, yet women who lead can advocate co-partnership rather than hierarchy (consistent with #8 in the first set of megatrends). Overbearing women create problems like those

created by overbearing men. On the other hand, women have tradition-
ally been socialized to accentuate interpersonal skills, which may give
them considerable potential for people-oriented, "high touch" leadership in religious education volunteer programs.

Naisbitt's comments on religious revival are most interesting. He suggests that the resurgence of fundamentalism (in many religious traditions, not just Christianity), the charismatic awakening, the New Age
Movement, and a general affirmation of spirituality may spell an age of
revival in the near future. Yet he notes that a recent Gallup poll found that,
while a large majority of Americans affirm the existence of God and the
importance of religion, they fail to find fulfillment in the local church:
Nearly half said they do not attend church, and well over half stated that
their churches were too concerned with organizational rather than spiritual issues. Unfortunately this can filter into religious education volunteer
programs as much as any other area of church work.

Naisbitt notes that programs for children fill an important need in religious education — most of the baby boomers who return to church do so,
at least in part, so that their children can obtain a religious education.
This emphasis upon children's religious education is underscored by a
number of other sources as well (see the Introduction to Donald Ratcliff's
Handbook of Children's Religious Education). In addition, there is greater
potential for religious education volunteerism as increasing numbers of
people return to church. While mainline churches have declined for some
time, Naisbitt sees them as having potential to grow again if they affirm
basics (such as conversion), become open to charismatics, and create
small groups for prayer and Bible study. Moreover, the church that is
responsive to people and their needs, especially their spiritual needs,
will receive the influx of returning baby boomers. Religious education volunteers can help meet those needs, if the volunteer ministry is flexible
enough to adapt rather than rigidly adhering to ministries that have been
useful in the past.

Naisbitt's final trend points to the increased emphasis upon the individual. He carefully distinguishes the new individualism from self-ori-
ented, sometimes selfish individualism of the past. Instead, the new individualism emphasizes personal responsibility which links consequences
with actions. He notes that people increasingly feel the need to change
themselves before society can be changed, because the basic unit of society is the individual. The implications for religious education volunteer
efforts are twofold. First, personal religious commitment is primary and
antecedent to effective religious education volunteerism. The spiritual

must be met first, as emphasized in the previous megatrend, which involves individual commitment. From that commitment comes responsibility for actions, including efforts to help others. Thus the second implication is that personal responsibility for one's time and energy should be affirmed and directed toward volunteer religious education work. Naisbitt notes that in the past personal responsibility has often been negated by people "hiding" within collective structures — "the government should be doing something" mentality. Church organizations have likewise provided a means of hiding from personal responsibility ("We hire the preacher/priest/religious education director/etc., to do the work"). We must not advocate this cloaked irresponsibility but rather affirm the personal responsibility of becoming involved in the church ministry of religious education, through volunteering. To quote Naisbitt, "The religious revival reflects a shift from the collective of organized religion to the individuality of faith. . . . Only individuals can experience the transcendent."

Trends in Volunteerism Suggested by George Barna

In his book *The Frog and the Kettle* religious researcher George Barna suggests that the values of society are changing from:
1. An emphasis upon money to an emphasis upon time
2. From commitment to flexibility
3. From the group to the individual
4. From work providing satisfaction to leisure producing satisfaction

All of these are important to using religious education volunteers effectively, hence most have been mentioned earlier in this book.

In a recent study Barna discovered that certain individuals are succumbing to heavy time demands and demonstrating less willingness to volunteer. People earning less than $20,000 annually, those without a high school education, Roman Catholics, and single people are tending to decrease the amount of time they volunteer. In contrast, those least inclined to reduce their volunteerism included those earning over $40,000, mainline Protestants, and college graduates. These may be important hints as to where religious education volunteer recruitment should be directed in the future, as well as what groups may need increased motivation to volunteer.

Barna's emphasis upon the increased value of time merits special attention. He notes that it is crucial to consider the high value people place on the time we ask them to give to the church. We must use that time wisely, regardless of whether they are directly participating or simply observing. If they begin to feel they are wasting their time (or we are wasting their time) they will lose interest and probably terminate their involvement. This is especially important in religious education volunteer efforts.

Like Naisbitt, Barna notes the universal shift from commitment to organizations. Loyalty and being a member of a group are far less important to people than previously. For example, the likelihood of joining a church has decreased for the last ten years because people want independence. They are only willing to commit themselves to tasks when they can expect results that exceed the amount of time they must sacrifice. Other indications of reduced commitment noted by Barna include:

1. The increase of people who do not show up after they have committed to attend an event
2. The number of people joining groups such labor unions, clubs, and so on have decreased
3. Loyalty to name brands has decreased
4. People report having fewer close friends

While we may rightly bemoan the reduction in the above areas of commitment, it is imperative for the church to foster religious education volunteerism efforts that will encourage commitment by appealing to their sometimes latent interests and perhaps unused abilities. Volunteers must gain a sense of ownership in the religious education enterprise, rather than seeing themselves as outsiders that tag along.

Barna also notes the high value placed upon gaining communication skills and insight into relationships. These should be a part of religious education volunteerism. This dovetails with Naisbitt's "high touch" emphasis in modern relationships. Furthermore, Barna describes the attractiveness of tangible outcomes from volunteer efforts for baby boomers. They demonstrate less interest in mindless activities such as watching television than other segments of the population. If they see concrete results from their religious education volunteer efforts, they will continue to volunteer and perhaps even expand their areas of involvement.

What lies in the future of volunteerism, according to Barna? People will willingly give of their time for volunteer efforts, but they will use greater selectivity in their decisions because of their limited amount of time. A key to involvement is, again, their observing some tangible result of their work. Because of their affluence, senior citizens and baby boomers can spend a greater percentage of their leisure time in religious education volunteerism efforts. The degree of involvement will be motivated by the relationships they develop, perception of making demonstrable change in the world and those around them, and reduction of stress. In other words, these measures of personal gain are the motivation that under-lies supposedly altruistic behavior.

Barna states that throughout the decade of the 1990s, those that vol-unteer will be driven more by specific causes, particularly political and social issues. The key is to orient religious education volunteer efforts toward these kinds of goals — that teaching religion provides a key to improving our world, both socially and spiritually. According to Barna, those who project the church as a means of changing society's values will have plenty of volunteers. Communication that is effective and cel-ebrating the specific results of volunteer projects are essential to this process.

Barna also emphasizes that plenty of individuals are skilled and able to be leaders in the church, but they generally do not want to shoulder that burden alone; they prefer a partnership ministry. Burnout of volunteers poses a problem, which means that limits should be placed on how long people serve with the option of reenlisting if they wish. Hands-on involve-ment in volunteer work helps people practice leadership, not just learn about it. Training must provide experience, not just talk.

In what areas can we expect to see the greatest growth of religious education volunteers? In his book *America 2000* Barna states that steady but slow growth can be expected in Bible study groups, home churches, and fellowship groups. People will increasingly participate selectively in the programs and events of the church. Fewer people will be involved because they feel an obligation, while only those activities that are of considerable interest will result in their participation. Elsewhere he emphasizes the need to involve the elderly in church volunteerism. Many elderly people want to work and are able to do so mentally and physically. Their main goal lies not in making money, but in taking on a challenge that provides fulfillment and being involved in a task that helps them per-ceive control over their lives.

Volunteers in Healthy, Growing Churches

Barna made a broad study of spiritually and numerically growing churches, detailed in his book *User-Friendly Churches*. By examining vol-unteerism in these churches, we may surmise additional details as to how religious education efforts can be most effective in the future. He notes that these churches tend to have many qualified, capable volun-teers. They emphasize the need to discover and use the gifts God gives individuals.

These healthy churches accept people as they are and find areas where they can effectively serve, rather than trying to fit people into the most needy area. These churches identified the talents of volunteers, helped them refine those talents, gave them opportunity to use those abilities, and supported them as they gave of their time. Disappointment and burnout were minimized by being sure they served in areas of interest and ability, resulting in a positive attitude about the church generally. These are certainly helpful guidelines to consider in religious education volunteerism as much as any other area of church volunteerism. What about areas of ministry for which there are no volunteers? These churches could quickly terminate areas of ministry that are not working or that have no volunteers. Growing churches begin new ministries when interested, skilled people show the need in those areas; growing churches take chances. As emphasized earlier, great churches are *people-driven*, not organization-driven. When a leader has little vision beyond the present needs of the church organization, there is little chance for vital, relevant ministry. Religious education volunteerism must constantly keep these guidelines at the forefront.

In healthy churches volunteers received the same esteem as professionals, which showed the importance of their efforts. Yet volunteers were also held accountable for their performance, which increased the respect volunteers held for the church. They realized that mediocrity was not an option. Accountability and respect are essential at all levels of the religious education lattice (see chapter four), two characteristics that help make a healthy church healthy.

The leadership in these churches was marked by a team approach, not individual leadership of volunteer efforts. Thus responsibility was shared and not dumped on one person. In addition, the church staff and pastor shared responsibilities with volunteers. Churches functioned as resources for volunteers, and providing access to resources became a central task for the staff. The staff watched for indications of burnout in volunteers, while unhealthy churches either fail to recognize those indications or they see them and then try to obtain every last bit of energy the volunteer has. In healthy churches burnout was avoided by planning sabbaticals when volunteers could renew their excitement and energy while others took their place. If some had been volunteering for some time, a break was encouraged by the church leaders.

In healthy churches, volunteers were carefully monitored and encouraged to avoid overcommitment. Leadership training at healthy churches involved helping people find and use their gifts. These churches helped leaders realize that serving others was a means of individual fulfillment, rather than concentrating upon the effect on the church. In other words, the perspective was that volunteers would benefit from involvement and training, not that the church would benefit. Relationships, not certificates and awards, were their rewards. Access to church resources (e.g., information) and staff also became rewards. Reinforcement always came in the context of groups, such as banquets, special desserts, etc.

Where Is Volunteerism Going?

From the Barna research, as well as the Naisbitt's megatrends, we can perhaps begin to visualize the outline for successful religious education volunteerism in the future.

Charles Colson in his article "Will the Church Miss the Volunteer Revolution?" notes a dramatic upswing of volunteerism in 1991 reported by a number of agencies. He cites Peter Drucker, a management specialist writing in the *Wall Street Journal*, who predicts that the number of volunteers will double by the end of the decade. Two-thirds of the population will be volunteering by the year 2000, up from the one-third at present, says Drucker. What accounts for the upswing and dramatic forecast? Drucker notes that nonprofit groups generally are far more efficient. Evidence for this conclusion includes parochial schools in New York which produce students with high achievement but cost only half that of the public schools and the Salvation Army's success in rehabilitating prisoners in Florida which markedly contrasts with dismal results of the prison system in that area that cost twice as much per person. Colson concludes that a key task of the church is to mobilize this coming influx of volunteers for religious efforts (including religious education).

One question yet unanswered is whether religious belief affects the degree of involvement in volunteerism. *Christianity Today* states that volunteerism is increasing in the United States. Religious belief is a key factor in this increase: 60 percent of church members volunteered their time. Those who attended weekly volunteered nearly three times as much as those who attend church occasionally, and they volunteered nearly twice as much time as those who did not attend church at all. Nearly half reported their religious beliefs as the major motivator for volunteering. African Americans have particularly increased their amount of volunteering.

Thus we conclude there is tremendous potential for religious education volunteerism in the future, if the local church adapts and directs its efforts in the most productive directions. The research cited in this chapter, as well as the guidelines presented throughout this book, attempt to outline the means to productive religious education volunteerism in future decades. Volunteerism in the world of the present and future will be and is quite unlike that of the past. The church must take hold of the opportunities in order to gain optimal productivity in religious education volunteer efforts.

For Further Reading

Barna, George. *America 2000*. Glendale, Calif.: Barna Research Associates, 1989.

Barna, George. *The Frog and the Kettle*. Ventura, Calif.: Regal, 1990.

Barna, George. *User-Friendly Churches*. Ventura, Calif.: Regal, 1991.

Barna, George. *What Americans Believe*. Ventura, Calif.: Regal, 1991.

Colson, Charles. "Will the Church Miss the Volunteer Revolution?" *Christianity Today* (9 March 1992), p. 88.

Naisbitt, John. *Megatrends*. New York: Warner Books, 1982. (Also see David McKenna's excellent application of this book to the church: *MegaTruth*. San Bernadino, Calif.: Here's Life, 1986.)

Naisbitt, John, and Patricia Aburdene. *Megatrends 2000*. New York: William Morrow, 1990.

Ratcliff, Donald, ed. *Handbook of Children's Religious Education*. Birmingham, Ala.: Religious Education Press, 1992.

"Religious Faith: Firm Foundation for Charity." *Christianity Today* (19 November 1990), p. 63.

Appendix

Where to Get More Information

MICHAEL A. SHARP

Volunteering and the motivations behind it need to be analyzed through good research. While there is limited data available that speaks directly to religious volunteerism, several organizations specialize in helping people learn how to obtain, screen, train, reward, and retain volunteers. Many of the principles and information can be adapted to religious education by directors of religious education. Following this list of organizations is a summary of religious research studies in volunteerism.

Volunteer Organizations

ARNOVA: Association for Research on Nonprofit Organizations and Voluntary Action
Barbara Long
Washington State University
Rt. 2, Box 696
Pullman, WA 99163
A national organization that provides members with an annual conference featuring workshops, panels, and paper sessions. All are geared to enhancing the field of volunteer work. This organization publishes Citizen Participation and Voluntary Action Abstracts and Nonprofit and Voluntary Sector Quarterly (previously titled Journal of Voluntary Action Research). ARNOVA was originally the Association of Voluntary Action Scholars in Medford, Massachusetts.

The Center For Volunteer Development
Virginia Tech
Blacksburg, VA 24061
(703) 961-7966
Supported by the Kellogg Foundation, this organization specializes in addressing questions relative to the development and training of volunteers and volunteer programs. It processes requests for assistance through the Virginia Cooperative Extension Program. This particular organization also sponsors a Volunteer Intern Program.

The Commission on Voluntary Service & Action (CVSA)
475 Riverside Dr. Room 933
New York, NY 10115
This organization provides a publication, *Volunteer!*, which serves as a comprehensive guide to voluntary services in the U.S. and other countries. Their publication lists upwards of 150 agencies.

Volunteer Management Program
University of Colorado
Office of Conference Services
Campus Box 454
Boulder, CO 80309
This program agency offers three levels of intensive, five-day workshops for volunteer managers. It also certifies volunteer administrators. This university has been serving the needs of volunteers and volunteer management since the early 1970s. The director, Marlene Wilson, has authored a number of excellent books on volunteers, some specifically oriented toward religious volunteer efforts.

Research on Religious Volunteerism

The following information was primarily gathered from the ERIC and PsycLitt databases (Spring 1991) and *Volunteerism: Motivational Theory and Research* (1990), a database of volunteer information developed by Eileen Starr. Her computer database [available from Trinity Evangelical Divinity School, Deerfield, IL] in the area of volunteers is extensive and further study of her work would benefit the reader greatly.

Allport, Gordon, and J. Michael Ross. "Personal religious orientation and prejudice." *Journal of Personality and Social Psychology* 5 (1967), pp. 432-443.

This work generates a clear understanding of the difference between intrinsic and extrinsic motivations. It focuses upon the relation of that motivation to religious work.

Ashdown, William. *Motivation and response in religion.* Glendale, Ohio: The Glenmary Department of Research, Glenmary Home Missions, 1962.

Catholics are surveyed as to their motivations for church attendance. Motivational needs and general views of religious motivation are discussed.

Backus, William. "A counseling center staffed by trained Christian lay persons. Special Issue: Lay Christian counseling." *Journal of Psychology and Christianity* 6:2 (Summer, 1987), pp. 39-44.

This church-based counseling center used trained, professionally supervised volunteers to produce changes in the spirituality, prayer and values of clients.

Bernt, Frank M. "Being religious and being altruistic: A study of college service volunteers." *Personality and Individual Differences* 10:6 (1989), pp. 663-669.

This study deals the approach to religion held by college students who volunteer. Those who volunteer seem to score higher in the area of intrinsic religiousness.

Cardenzana, Victor Felix. *Sources of satisfaction and dissatisfaction for volunteer religious education school instructors.* Ed.D. dissertation, University of Cincinnati, 1976.

This test of the Motivator-Hygiene theory investigated the satisfaction or lack thereof of religious education volunteers. The article gives pertinent information on both dependent and independent variables of satisfaction.

Collins, Gary. *Man in motion, the psychology of human motivation.* Carol Stream, Ill.: Creation House, 1973.

Need reduction theory serves as the hingepin for this study of what causes behavior. The specific impetus of this research was exploring reasons why people are active in church.

Donahue, Michael J. "Intrinsic and extrinsic religiousness: Review and meta-analysis." *Journal of Personality and Social Psychology* 48:2 (1985), pp. 400-419.

This study reviews literature relative to intrinsic and extrinsic motivations of those who are religious. The study suggests degrees of satisfaction for intrinsic reasons are related to degrees of conservativism.

Hartley, Loyde Hobart. *Sectarianism and social participation: A study of the relationship between religious attitudes and involvement in voluntary organizations in seventy-two churches in the southern Appalachian mountains.* Ph.D. dissertation, Emory University, Atlanta, Ga., 1968.
This study examines how elements of sectarianism affect involvement in secular and church-related volunteer organizations. One aspect of sectarianism, the tendency toward isolation, was related to noninvolvement in volunteer work, but not other components.

Hendrix, Richard. *Motivation of the volunteer worker in the local church.* M.A. thesis, Trinity Evangelical Divinity School, Deerfield, IL., 1974.
Motivation is defined in relation to church volunteers, emphasizing both standard theories and spiritual aspects of motivation (such as influence by the Holy Spirit).

Keyser, Albert W. "Legal guardianship for the elderly: A volunteer model." *Journal of Religion and Aging* 2:4 (Summer, 1986), pp. 41-46.
A volunteer guardianship program for Lutheran Ministers of Florida uses the teamwork approach for aiding dependent adults who have been judged incompetent. Both professional staff and the volunteers meet the needs of patients on the ward.

Lazerwitz, Bernard. Membership in voluntary associations and frequency of church attendance. *Journal for the Scientific Study of Religion* 2 (1967), pp. 74-84.
This article considers how church attendance relates to involvement in volunteer efforts. Membership in organizations is related to frequency of attendance for Catholics and Protestants.

McDonough, Reginald, and George Hearn. *Motivation of volunteer workers*. Research project 059, Phase II, Report Vol. C. Nashville: The Sunday School Board of the Southern Baptist Convention, 1969.

   Research of 427 churches revealed that participating in training, witnessing, and worship are related to positive motivation toward volunteering. Specific motivations included a sense of calling, wanting to help others in a religious life, wanting to help people learn about God, and love for others.

McDonough, Reginald, and George Hearn. *Motivation of volunteer workers*. Research project 059, Phase II, Report Vol. D. Nashville: The Sunday School Board of the Southern Baptist Convention, 1969.

   This study of 375 volunteers in church contexts found that volunteers become involved because of self-esteem needs. Key motivations include pressure from others, spiritual factors, and leadership. Service was related to self-fulfillment, status, desire for growth, and desire to be with others.

Paget, Virginia Marks. *Commitment of volunteers and the work of the church*. Ph.D. dissertation, Washington University, St. Louis, Missouri, 1982.

   The perception of self during activities was found to motivate individuals in seven church-oriented groups.

Sherman, J. Daniel, and Howard L. Smith. "The influence of organizational structure on intrinsic versus extrinsic motivation." *Academy of Management Journal* 27:4 (1984), pp. 877-885.

   Six Protestant denominations contributed to this study of the effect of organizational structure on motivations in volunteerism. Church size was a factor in motivation.

Spilka, Bernard, Phillip Shaver, and Lee Kirkpatrick. "A general attribution theory for the psychology of religion." *Journal for the Scientific Study of Religion* 24 (1985), pp. 1-118.

   The needs for sense of meaning, for control over life happenings, and for self esteem are seen as the impetus for individual involvement in religion. This study maintains that these factors contribute to an individual's day-to-day interpretation of events and to ascription of cause and meaning.

ADDITIONAL REFERENCES

Arthur, Julietta. *Retire to Action: A Guide to Volunteer Service*. Nashville: Abingdon, 1969.

Barna, George. *The Barna Report 1992-93*. Ventura, Calif.: Regal. [See tables 97-99 on pp. 280-282 regarding church volunteers.]

Bill, J. Brent. "Make Your Volunteers a Winning Team." *Group* 14:1 (November/December 1987), pp. 8-9.

Christie, Les. "In Search of Volunteers." *Group* 14:7 (September 1988), pp. 8-11.

Custer, Chester. "The Church's Ministry and the Coming of the Aged." *Circuit Rider* (September 1991), pp. 4-6.

Engstrom, Ted, and Edward Dayton. "Volunteers - Bane or Blessing?" *Christian Leadership Letter* (May 1986).

Gales, Danny. "Disarming Tensions Between Paid Staff and Volunteers." *Preacher's Magazine* (March-May 1985).

Geaney, Dennis. *Full Church, Empty Rectories: Training Lay Ministers for Parishes Without Priests*. Notre Dame, Ind.: Fides/Claretian Press, 1980.

Halverson, Delia. *How to Train Volunteer Teachers*. Nashville: Cokesbury, 1990.

Hendee, John. *Recruiting, Training and Developing Volunteer Adult Workers*. Cincinnati: Standard, 1988.

Henlin, Arthur. "A Program for Recruiting and Involving Laymen and Laywomen for Ministry in Apostle United Presbyterian Church, West Allis, Wis." Doctor of Ministries project. Deerfield, Ill.: Trinity Evangelical Divinity School, 1984.

Heusser, D. B. *Helping Church Workers Succeed: The Enlistment and Support of Volunteers*. Valley Forge, Pa.: Judson, 1980.

Johnson, Douglas. *The Care and Feeding of Volunteers*. Nashville: Abingdon, 1978.

Leckey, Dolores. "The Challenge of Lay Ministry Formation." In *Christian Adulthood: A Catechetical Resource*, ed. Neil Parent, pp. 33-35. Washington, D.C.: U.S.C.C. Publications, 1983.

Loth, Paul. "How to Involve Volunteers in Church Ministry." *Christian Education Today* (Fall 1985).

Monroe, Theresa. "Educational Aspects of Lay Ministry." In *Growing Together: A Conference on Shared Ministry*, ed. M. B. Mathieson, pp. 58-66. Washington, D.C.: U.S.C.C. Publications, 1980.

Morris, Margie. *Volunteer Ministries: New Strategies for Today's Church*. Sherman, Tex.: Newton-Cline Press, 1990.

National Center for Citizen Involvement. *Religion and Volunteering*. Boulder, Colo.: NCCI, 1978.

Office of Church Life and Leadership, United Church of Christ. *The Ministry of Volunteers.* Winston-Salem, N.C.: OCLL/UCC, 1979.

Oswald, Roy, with Jackie McMakin. *How to Prevent Lay Leader Burnout.* Washington, D.C.: Alban Institute, 1984.

Roehlkepartain, Eugene. *Building Bridges: Teens in Community Service.* Minneapolis: RespecTeen/Lutheran Brotherhood, 1991.

Roehlkepartain, Eugene. *The Teaching Church.* Nashville: Abingdon, 1993.

Scheitlin, G. E., et al. *Recruiting and Developing Volunteer Leaders.* Philadelphia: Parish Life Press, 1979.

Schorr, Vernie. *Recruiting, Training and Developing Volunteer Children's Workers.* Cincinnati: Standard, 1990.

Senter III, Mark. "Principles of Leadership Recruitment." In *Christian Education: Foundations for the Future,* ed. Robert Clark et al., pp. 469-479. Chicago: Moody, 1991.

Smith, David. "Churches are Generally Ignored in Voluntary Action Research." *Review of Religious Research* 24 (1983), pp. 295-303. Also see his article "Churches are Generally Ignored in Contemporary Voluntary Action Research." *Journal of Voluntary Action Research / Nonprofit and Voluntary Services Quarterly* 13:4 (1984), pp. 11-18.

Stone, David, and Rose Miller. *Volunteer Youth Workers.* Loveland, Colo.: Group, 1985.

Stringer, Peter. "A Comparison of Parish Councils and Voluntary Organizations." *Journal of Voluntary Action Research / Nonprofit and Voluntary Services Quarterly* 10:2 (1981), pp. 62-70.

United Church of Christ, Office of Church Life and Leadership. *Ministry of Volunteers: A Guidebook for Churches* (seven manuals). Arlington, Va.: Volunteer the National Center.

Williams, Charles, and Hilda Williams. "Contemporary Voluntary Associations in the Urban Black Church." *Journal of Voluntary Action Research / Nonprofit and Voluntary Sector Quarterly* 13:4 (1984), pp. 19-30.

Youthworker 2:4 (Winter 1986), pp. 16-53. [Special issue devoted to volunteers among church youth. Includes articles by Anthony Campolo, Greg McKinnan, Scott Koenigsaecker, David Olshine, and others.]

For information on conferences and/or updates on religious education volunteerism, write: Donald Ratcliff, Box 800840, Toccoa Falls, GA 30598.

Index of Names

241

Index of Subjects